The

CRAFT
BEER
COOKBOOK

FROM IPAS AND BOCKS TO PILSNERS AND PORTERS

The

CRAFT
BEER
COOKBOOK

100 ARTISANAL RECIPES
FOR COOKING WITH BEER

Jacquelyn Dodd

adamsmedia
Avon, Massachusetts

Published by
Adams Media, a division of F+W Media, Inc.
57 Littlefield Street, Avon, MA 02322. U.S.A.
www.adamsmedia.com

ISBN 10: 1-4405-6491-4
ISBN 13: 978-1-4405-6491-8
eISBN 10: 1-4405-6492-2
eISBN 13: 978-1-4405-6492-5

Printed in the United States of America.

10 9 8 7 6 5 4 3

Library of Congress Cataloging-in-Publication Data
Dodd, Jacquelyn.
  The craft beer cookbook / Jacquelyn Dodd.
      pages cm
  Includes bibliographical references and index.
  ISBN 978-1-4405-6491-8 (alkaline paper) -- ISBN 1-4405-6491-4 (alk. paper) --
ISBN 978-1-4405-6492-5 (electronic) --   ISBN 1-4405-6492-2 (electronic)
1. Cooking (Beer) I. Title.
  TX726.3.D63 2013
  641.6'23--dc23

2013013872

Photographs by Jacquelyn Dodd.

Cover images © *www.clipart.com*.

This book is available at quantity discounts for bulk purchases.
For information, please call 1-800-289-0963.

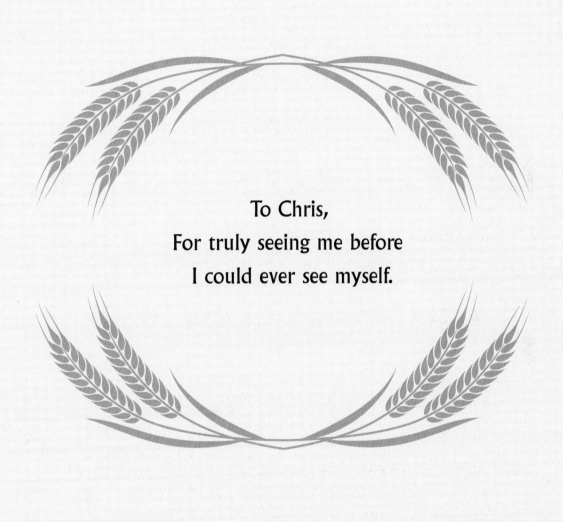

To Chris,
For truly seeing me before
I could ever see myself.

THE THANK YOUS & SUCH

IT TAKES A VILLAGE TO WRITE A BOOK. Although only my name appears on the cover, there are a number of people who deserve far more credit for the creation of this book than they could ever receive. Chris, possibly the best example of a human you could ever come across, for being more than an entire support system all on his own. Claire, for being my motivation and inspiration, as well as turning me into the best part of who I am. Cori, for being an incredible sister and best friend, teaching me to make cereal on the kitchen floor when I was three years old, and all the things that symbolized. Kim, for logic and sarcasm in equal measure exactly when I need it. Tara, for being one of the strongest people I know. Mom, for always underscoring the importance of gratitude and generosity. Dino, for not only negotiating this book deal, but for being the very first person to introduce me to the joy of remarkable food. Ross at Adams Media for understanding my vision and the respect I have for craft beer and its people. For brewers everywhere, who keep me hooked on the flavors and inspired to keep creating beer-infused food.

I also owe an enormous debt of gratitude to the recipe testers. About two months into the process of writing this cookbook, I put a small posting on my website. A mere wondering: Would anyone be willing to make one or two of these recipes and send me some feedback? Can you help a girl out? I wanted to ensure not only that the recipes worked, but also that they were worth making. The response was overwhelming. Within an hour my inbox was full of messages from volunteers. College students with little more than a dorm stove, single moms, retirees, newlyweds wanting to learn to cook, professional chefs, and food bloggers all wanted to help me out. It nearly brought me to tears: the selflessness of the gesture from so many strangers. Now if you find that a recipe works—and the cocoa powder isn't missing from the instructions—and I actually list when to add the beer—it's probably because of one of these people:

Coreen Wilson, Kim van Groos, Maggie Lynch, Ashley Manila, Carlie Maridakis, Ashley Reyer, Katie Hanzlik, Sam Ellis, Chef Christopher Cody, Carrie Parks-Gomes, Addie K Martin, Becky Gerard, Maggie Price, Jessica Hudak, Jeremiah Ramey, Christina Dey, Jessica Miller, Tyler Hackett, Jessica Mahoney, Kristi Kaiser, Cathy Burke, Dervla Kelly, Sarah MacDonald, Nicole Birks, Natalie Wiser-Orozco from *The Devil Wears Parsley*, Julie Pollock, Jill Marlin, Brie Hilkin, Anna Burr, Deb Beaverson, Emily Boimare, Vicki Hoiten, Brigid Jennings, Karen Skinner, David Olson, Christa Lewandowski, Amber Hanna Forbes, Ariana Ziskin, Jay D. Bennett.

So please, on my behalf, if you meet some of them, buy them a beer. They deserve it.

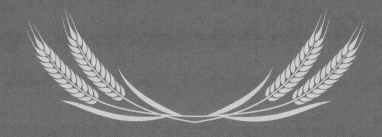

CONTENTS

Introduction 12
Beer 101: Beer Style Basics 14
Cooking with Beer 18

Chapter 1
BREAKFAST ... 24

Amber Ale Pecan Cinnamon Rolls
with Beer Cream Cheese Frosting [M] . . . 26

Apple Cheddar Beer Pancakes . . . 28

Beer and Buttermilk Biscuits . . . 30

Chocolate Stout French Toast Casserole . . . 31

Chocolate Chip and Smoked Porter
Pancakes . . . 33

Croque Madame with Beer Cheese Sauce . . . 34

Orange Wheat Beer and Dark Chocolate
Muffins [M] . . . 36

Wheat Beer Dutch Babies . . . 37

Sausage and Pale Ale Frittata . . . 38

Pale Ale Corn Waffles with Scrambled
Eggs and Smoky Beer Cheese Sauce . . . 40

Chapter 2
APPETIZERS, STARTERS, AND SIDES ... 42

Baked Brie with Amber Ale–Caramelized
Apples and Pancetta . . . 44

Beer-Braised Green Beans with
Bacon and Shallots . . . 46

Beer Grits with Goat Cheese and Chives . . . 47

Beer Cheese Gratin Potatoes . . . 49

Chili Con Queso Cerveza Crostini . . . 50

IPA Guacamole [M] . . . 51

Jalapeños and Bacon Beer Cheese Dip . . . 52

Roasted Garlic IPA Hummus [H] . . . 53

Porter Caramelized Onion Dip [M] . . . 54

Roasted Garlic Pale Ale
Whipped Potatoes [H] . . . 56

Soft Pretzels with Chipotle
Beer Cheese Sauce . . . 57

Chapter 3
SAUCES ... 60

Amber Ale Caramel Sauce . . . 62

Chocolate Stout Fudge Sauce [H] . . . 63

Creamy Pale Ale Basil Pesto Sauce [M] . . . 64

Foolproof Beer Cheese Sauce . . . 65

IPA Puttanesca Sauce [M] . . . 66

IPA Honey Mustard Vinaigrette [H] . . . 69

Orange Hefeweizen Marmalade . . . 71

Maple Stout Barbecue Sauce . . . 73

Porter Fig Jam . . . 74

Stout-Balsamic Glaze . . . 75

Chapter 4
BREADS AND PASTAS...76

Belgian White Ale English Muffin Loaf Bread . . . 78

Chocolate, Bacon, and Porter Muffins . . . 79

Classic Beer Bread . . . 80

Drunken Carbonara Couscous . . . 81

Hefeweizen Brioche Pull-Apart
Dinner Roll Loaf . . . 82

Loaded Beer Corn Bread . . . 84

Pale Ale Corn Tortillas . . . 85

Pale Ale Pasta Cavatelli . . . 86

Pumpkin IPA Scones [M] . . . 89

Roasted Garlic and Cheddar
Beer Cheese Muffins . . . 90

Pasta with Arugula, Tomatoes, and
a Lemon-Beer Cream Sauce . . . 92

Smoky Beer Mac and Cheese . . . 94

Wheat Beer Sesame Hamburger Buns . . . 96

Chapter 5
VEGGIE-LOVERS ENTRÉES...98

Irish Red Ale Butternut Squash Bisque
with Goat Cheese and Pomegranate . . . 100

Porter Black Bean Soup with
Avocado Cilantro Cream . . . 103

Pale Ale Caprese Pizza . . . 104

Roasted Mushroom and Brown Ale Soup . . . 106

Mushroom Stout Sliders with
Chipotle Cream . . . 108

Saison Ricotta, Roasted Tomatoes, and
Porter-Caramelized Shallots Galette . . . 109

Chapter 6
BEEF AND PORK...112

Beer-Braised Pulled-Pork Tacos with
Beer Corn Tortillas . . . 115

Beer-Braised Short Rib Sliders with
Quick Pickled Slaw . . . 117

Steak with Stout Portobello
Mushroom Sauce . . . 118

Beer-Marinated Flank Steak with IPA
Chimichurri [M] . . . 119

Chorizo Stout Sloppy Joes . . . 121

IPA-Marinated Pork Chops with Stout
Cherry Sauce . . . 122

Pig Newton Beer Burger . . . 123

Porter-Braised Pulled-Pork Sandwiches with
IPA Jalapeño Slaw [M] . . . 126

Porter Osso Buco . . . 129

Slow-Roasted Maple Stout Baby Back
Beef Ribs . . . 130

Stout and Stilton Beef Empanadas . . . 133

Porter, Goat Cheese, and Portobello
Mushroom–Stuffed Pork Loin . . . 135

Chapter 7
THINGS WITH WINGS...136

Beer-Braised Chipotle Chicken with Red Peppers
over Drunken Cilantro Lime Rice . . . 138

Beer Marinara Turkey Meatball
Sandwiches . . . 140

Brown Ale–Brined Roast Turkey . . . 142

Brown Sugar and Brown Ale Niçoise
Chicken Thighs . . . 144

Honey Mustard Pale Ale Chicken . . . 146

Beer-Brined Salt-Roasted Chicken . . . 147

Paprika Chicken with Roasted Red Pepper Cream Sauce [M] . . . 148

Porter-Glazed Asian Chicken Meatballs . . . 150

Stout and Cheddar Chicken Potpie . . . 152

White Bean and Beer Chicken Chili . . . 153

Stout and Pomegranate–Glazed Chicken Wings . . . 154

Chapter 8
SEAFOOD . . . 156

Beer and Butter Garlic Prawns . . . 158

Beer-Brined Prosciutto–Wrapped Scallops with Stout Balsamic Glaze . . . 159

IPA Crab Cakes with Spicy Beer Hollandaise . . . 162

Lobster, Corn, and Beer Chowder . . . 165

IPA Watermelon Ceviche [H] . . . 169

Pilsner Coconut Curry Shrimp Soup . . . 171

Maple and Bourbon Barrel-Aged Beer–Glazed Salmon . . . 172

Salmon with Dijon Beer Cream Sauce over Drunken Couscous . . . 174

Chapter 9
DESSERTS . . . 176

Amber Ale Carrot Cake with Orange Mascarpone Filling and Beer-Spiked Cream Cheese Frosting [M] . . . 179

Chocolate Porter Fudge Cookies . . . 181

Chocolate Stout Brownies . . . 182

Lemon Orange IPA Pudding with Beer Whipped Cream [M] . . . 183

Chocolate Stout Cake with Chocolate Raspberry Ganache and Whipped Cream [M] . . . 184

Strawberry Pale Ale Popsicles [H] . . . 187

Chocolate Stout Ice Cream with Pretzels . . . 188

Chocolate Stout Mousse with Stout-Soaked Cherries [H] . . . 190

Frosted Vanilla Beer Butter Cookies [M] . . . 192

IPA Apple Fritters with Amber Ale Caramel Sauce . . . 195

IPA Pavlova with Beer Lemon Curd, Strawberries, and Beer Whipped Cream [M] . . . 196

Lemon Pilsner Cheesecake with Beer Lemon Curd . . . 198

Pale Ale Pastry Dough . . . 201

Lime IPA Granita with Candied Basil [H] . . . 203

Saison Caramelized Apple Cake with Beer Whipped Cream [M] . . . 204

Tropical IPA Fruit Tart . . . 206

Vegan Pumpkin Loaf Cake [M] . . . 208

Chocolate-Chip Stout Milk Shake [H] . . . 209

Appendix: Glossary of Beer Terms . . . 210
Index . . . 218

[H] **High Alcohol Warning** *(High levels of alcohol are still present.)*

[M] **Mild Alcohol Warning** *(One or more components contain small amounts of uncooked alcohol.)*

INTRODUCTION

Over the past decade there has been an explosion of well-made beer in the United States, a phenomenon we like to call the Craft Beer Movement. From home brewers to craft breweries, the United States is setting new records for beer production each year, with nearly 3,000 craft breweries. But what is *craft beer?* The definition is a bit wily and hard to pin down. The answer, more or less, is thoughtfully made beer using premium ingredients—beer made with a focus on quality over quantity and taste over profit. The enthusiasm these brewers have for their creations is infectious, erasing all stereotypes of a "beer scene" centered around keg stands, beer pong, and cold pizza. The craft beer movement is about taste, quality ingredients, years of shaping the perfect stout, the fine balance between hops and malt, and the resulting masterpiece. The first head brewer I ever met summed it up this way: "Good beer makes you think."

Cooking with beer isn't just a novelty; beer has exceptional powers in the kitchen. This book is filled with recipes that highlight the three main reasons to cook with beer: leavening, tenderizing, and taste.

Leavening is an incredible example of why beer is a fantastic baking ingredient. Because beer is brewed with so many of the same ingredients used to make breads, it's an excellent choice when baking. Beer is also a powerful meat tenderizer, giving even the toughest cuts of meat a texture makeover. And beer can lend its fantastic flavors to almost every kind of food there is. Once you pop a pint into that stew pot, you may never cook in a sober kitchen again.

Over the years of running a website centered on cooking with beer, TheBeeroness.com, I've become acquainted with beer of every type and how to integrate it into food. I've learned the perils of trying to reduce an IPA as well as the joys of baking a malty stout cake. This book draws on the lessons I've learned to find the perfect balance of beer flavor as well as the key to heighten beer's leavening and tenderizing properties. If you're new to beer, the Beer 101 section gives you a brief overview of the main beer styles so that you can get more familiar with the language. In the Cooking with Beer section, you will learn how to choose the right beer for cooking, how to amend your favorite existing recipes to include beer, and how to increase or decrease the level of beer flavor in your final results. For each recipe I've included Choose the Right Brew! sidebars to help you find the beer that goes best with each dish. So pour yourself a pint, grab a whisk, and let's get started!

BEER 101:
BEER STYLE BASICS

Here's a very quick and dirty intro to the most common styles of beer. This is not meant to be comprehensive, just a mere introduction; many great beer styles were not included. At the very top of the beer family tree, there are two main types of beer from which each style of beer descends: ales and lagers. Craft beer, like most great art, has begun to blur the lines of those two styles to produce hybrids. For our purposes, however, all beers are either one or the other. The difference, more or less, lies in the yeast.

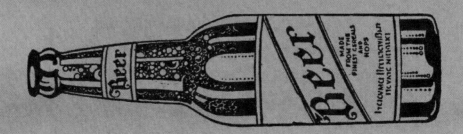

Ales

Although it's nearly impossible to pinpoint an actual beer birthday, ales came first and are thought to have graced the world with fermented goodness for as long as 9,000 years. Ales are what's known as "top fermented," which means the yeast rises to the top as the beer is created. Ales are fermented at higher temperatures and are commonly thought of as more full-bodied and more complex than lagers.

PALE ALES

Pale ales get their name from the pale malt used to make them, but they can range in color from a very light yellow to amber. Typically, a pale ale has an evenly balanced malt-to-hop ratio, so although the hop flavor is present, it's more subtle.

With that in mind, American pale ales, also known as American IPAs or American Indian pale ales, aren't shy with the hops. American brewers love their hops—in fact, the more the merrier—and they aren't afraid to add a double or even a triple dose for your drinking pleasure. "The more the merrier" is how America views its unabashed love of all things hops and in beer's equivalent of an arms race, they're in to create the hoppiest beer ever invented. If you grab yourself an American pale ale, brace yourself for a mouthful of hop flavor.

English Indian pale ales, or IPAs, while still hop-forward in taste, are more balanced than the American IPAs and tend to have an earthier, spicier quality. England is actually credited with the invention of the IPA, although beer geeks debate why. Some are quick to tell you that the IPA was invented out of necessity; the higher level of hops and alcohol allowed the beer to make the long voyage from England to India without spoiling. Others will argue that English brewers believed that hops were a necessity in warm climates. Either way, I love to sit back and watch a good, well-educated, beer debate. Pass me an IPA and I'll enjoy the show.

BROWN ALES

While the IPA is all about the hops, brown ales favor the malt. Brown ales range in color from amber to a rich chocolate and often lean toward flavors of nuts, caramel, and even fruit. Although brown ale is traditionally a low-hop beer, American brewers have often had their hoppy way with this style, and the traditional profile of the beer has changed in recent years. If a beer is labeled "American Brown Ale," count on more hops. If it's an "English Brown Ale," bet on a sweeter, maltier flavor.

PORTERS AND STOUTS

These are the dark knights of the beer world. Although the difference between the two is becoming increasingly blurred as the creativity and ingenuity of brewers continues to muddy the definitions of beer styles, there are a few things that most craft beer aficionados agree upon. First, stouts tend to use roasted barley, while porters generally don't. Second, porters tend to be a bit hoppier than stouts. Third, porters came first. The "stout porter," later shortened to just "stout," was conceived later, when someone decided to start tinkering with the porter's ABV (Alcohol by Volume, a standard measure of the alcohol content of a beverage). Finally, while there will always be argument over proper classification, someone will always be around to enjoy a pint!

WHEAT ALES

We give Germany the credit for these brews, which can range in color from very pale yellow to orange. Wheat beers are brewed with wheat and tend to have a yeast-forward taste and traditionally a lower hop profile. These beers often have flavor notes of banana, cloves, yeast, bread, and even bubble gum. The most common types of wheat beers are the popular hefeweizen and the Belgian white ale. Although some wheat beers can be bottom-fermented lagers, wheat beers are most commonly top-fermented ales.

Lagers

||||||||||||||||||||||||||||||||||||||||||||||||||||||||||||||||||||||||||||||||||||||||||||||||||||||||||||||||||||||||||||

Lagers are mere babies in comparison to good ol' ale, making an appearance on the beer scene in the early nineteenth century. If you grew up in the United States and had your first beer courtesy of a keg party hosted near the back of a pickup truck, there is a good chance you cut your beer-drinking teeth on a lager. Since ales are top fermented, you've probably already guessed that lagers are bottom fermented, which means the yeast settles to the bottom during fermentation. Lager fermentation takes place at colder temperatures, which generally means it takes longer. Lagers are known for their clean, crisp taste and are typically served at colder temperatures than ales.

PILSNER

The origins of this style go back to Pilsen in the Czech Republic, where this style of beer began in 1842 and is still produced today. Although a pilsner's flavor profile favors hops over malt, the pilsner's hops whisper rather than scream. Pilsners range in color from light straw to golden yellow.

PALE LAGERS

Although this is a beer style that is very rarely brewed by microbreweries or home brewers, it is the most widely consumed beer style in the world. It's a staple of large macro-breweries, characterized by its pale color as well as low hop and malt profiles. Pale lagers are often described as clean and crisp with no single ingredient's flavor taking center stage. It's a common practice for American macro-breweries to brew pale lagers using "adjacent" grains such as rice and corn.

BOCK

Bock beers range in color from a light amber to a deep caramel and have a slightly higher alcohol content than other lagers. Although traditionally viewed as a malty beer, many varieties of bock beer can have a very hop-forward taste profile. Bocks tend to be stronger and more full flavored than most lagers. They are often brewed for consumption in the spring as well as for celebrations.

COOKING WITH BEER

Choosing a beer for a recipe isn't as arbitrary as it may appear. It isn't very difficult, but it does require thought and planning. Substituting your favorite beer in a recipe isn't always a good idea; in fact, it may result in an end product that is nowhere near what you set out to accomplish. Let's take a quick look at some common questions and answers.

Where do I start? The recipe or the beer?

A: A fair question, and it's a toss-up. Whichever path you choose to start your beer-cooking adventure, the recipe or the beer, be mindful of the flavors. In general, dark beers go well with "dark" recipes. If that beer you want to bake with is a stout, look for a recipe that calls for "dark" (or "heavy") ingredients: chocolate, plums, bacon, and so forth. If the beer you love is a pilsner, look for a recipe with "light" ingredients: lemon, vanilla, fish, and so forth. The bottom line: Make sure the flavors of that beer you are about to pour into that stockpot match those of the dish. For instance, if you're making a chicken noodle soup, look for a beer with notes of citrus and herbs and not one with notes of coffee and caramel. There is some room to play around with this rule once you're familiar with the process, but finding complementary flavors is the key to success when cooking and baking with beer.

If you prefer to start with the recipe, then make note of the flavors and try to find a beer that mimics those. If you want to bake a chocolate dessert, for example, look for a beer with notes of chocolate, coffee, or malt. Look at the list of the beer's flavor notes and try to imagine those in your dish. Does that dish have dates, molasses, and nuts? Or does it have orange and rosemary notes? Look for a beer with similar flavors. Most large chain retailers of craft beer have cards near each beer that explain the flavor notes; these cards will give you a fairly accurate flavor profile. If you are making chili, for instance, you might look for a beer with notes of spice, smoke, and molasses.

Be careful with IPAs, recognized for their hoppy flavors. It's much more difficult to cook with high-hop beers due to the fact that the hops reduce to a very harsh, bitter product. Whenever a recipe calls for reducing beer, skip the IPA.

On the other hand, IPAs work well with strong starches and sugar, which tend to mellow the bitterness. They can also be used as a braising or soaking liquid when you want a stronger beer flavor. Because of this, IPA is also a great choice when a recipe calls for very little beer and you want a bigger beer flavor.

What about amending my favorite recipes? Can't I just substitute beer for some other liquid and call it a day?

A: Wouldn't that be nice? There are a few things to keep in mind when substituting beer for the liquid in an existing recipe. Let's start with baking. Beer makes an excellent liquid when baking cakes or making bread from scratch due to the fact that it is a mild leavening agent, so your baked goods get a great texture. However, since beer is usually fat free, each time you replace heavy cream, whole milk, or buttermilk in a cake recipe, you also remove fat.

Consequently, you will need to make up for that difference by adding oil or an extra egg yolk. A good rule of thumb is that for each ½ cup of fatty liquid you plan to replace with beer, add 1 tablespoon of oil to a ½ cup measuring cup (so 2 tablespoons for 1 cup, or 3 tablespoons for 1½ cups, you get the idea) and then fill the remaining space with beer. So your final substitution will be ½ cup fatty liquid replaced by ½ cup beer (minus 1 tablespoon) plus 1 tablespoon oil.

Bitterness is also a factor to consider as you amend a recipe. While most beer lovers will write sonnets about the wonderful palate caress of a well-bittered beer, it isn't the same while cooking. This doesn't mean you have to abandon the more bitter beers; they just take some finesse. Even in savory dishes, a bit of sweetness (e.g., molasses, honey, or even fruit juice) can help tame those unpleasant cooked flavors.

Keep in mind that the longer the beer reduces, the more intense and bitter it becomes. Of course, this can also work to your advantage. If you want to up the beer flavor, look for beers with high IBUs (International Bittering Units, a standard measurement for how bitter a beer is). The higher the IBU, the more intense the beer flavor will be. For better or for worse, those high-hop beers will give you a stronger beer flavor once cooked.

Another factor when cooking with beer involves the level of spice. Alcohol, in general, intensifies it. Keep that in mind when making sauces and braising spicy meat. You might want to pull back a bit on that cayenne or chipotle until you know how the beer's ABV (Alcohol by Volume) is going to affect your dish.

So I made my dish, and I wasn't happy with the level of beer flavor. What can I do to fix this next time?

A: If the beer flavor was too intense, you have two options. First, and most obviously, use less beer. You can replace some of it with water, milk, or both. Second, you can try a less intense beer. A more mellow, lower-hop beer will give you a lower final beer flavor. Try a saison, a pilsner, or a hefeweizen.

Now, if the beer flavors didn't come through as strongly as you had hoped, there are a few tricks to try next time:

🌿 You can add more beer. However, adding more liquid will probably require you to rebalance the rest of the recipe.

🌿 You can also try a beer with more hops. Just remember that this may cause an intense bitterness. The results will depend on exactly what level of beer kick to the mouth you are looking for.

You can also try reducing by half the beer that you plan to add to the recipe. This works especially well with malty, low-hop beers, such as stouts, porters, and even wheat beers. For instance, if the recipe calls for ½ cup beer, start by placing 1 cup of beer in a pot over medium-high heat. Bring it to a boil and then stir it occasionally until it reduces to ½ cup, cooling if necessary.

The last wild and crazy idea is to make a beer extract. Pour a bottle of beer into a pot on a stove over medium-high heat. Stir it occasionally, and don't stop cooking it until it has reduced to 1 or 2 teaspoons of a thick glaze. This creates a beer extract that can give that beer punch without adding excessive amounts of liquid to your dish.

On the next page is a chart to get you started. While these are not hard-and-fast rules for beer cooking success, they're an excellent jumping-off point. Just remember that each beer is created differently, and brewers are becoming more adventurous when it comes to experimenting with ingredients. Consequently, it is even more important to respect the flavor notes in each bottle or can that you want to cook with.

Does the alcohol cook off?

A: You might be asking this question so that you can serve a dish to an underage guest, or maybe so you don't get Grandma sloshed by accident at Thanksgiving dinner. Or you may want to know if it's a quick way for you to get sloshed at Thanksgiving dinner. Either way, it's a great question, and I wish I possessed a simple answer to it.

For years it was widely accepted that alcohol burns off during cooking. But how long does food need to be cooked for this to happen? And at what temperature? The answers are still being debated, but the consensus is that some small amounts of alcohol will still remain even after hours of cooking.

That said, these amounts are normally so insignificant that their effects will not be felt. As a result, at restaurants you can order steak in a red wine sauce or a rum raisin cake without being carded. Similarly, it's legal for restaurants to serve dishes cooked with alcohol to minors because the amount of alcohol left behind is so minute.

In order for the beer to be cooked enough to remove the majority of the alcohol it must be cooked at 178°F (or above) for at least 10 minutes. This isn't much. Nearly everything that is baked will meet these requirements. Pan-fried items generally will also meet the requirements, and although beer-battered foods aren't cooked for 10 minutes, the

	APPLES, PEARS, PEACHES	BREAD, PASTA	CHOCOLATE	CITRUS	SEAFOOD	RED MEAT	WHITE MEAT	SQUASH, ROOT VEGETABLES
STOUT Colors: Dark brown to black Flavors: Chocolate, Coffee, Malt			✓			✓		
PORTER Color: Dark brown Flavors: Chocolate, Coffee, Date			✓			✓		
BROWN ALE Colors: Light to medium brown Flavors: Chocolate, Nuts, Caramel						✓	✓	✓
AMBER ALE Colors: Amber to red Flavors: Caramel, Toasted Malt, Fruit	✓					✓	✓	✓
PILSNER Colors: Light to medium yellow Flavors: Floral, Citrus, Hops	✓	✓		✓	✓		✓	✓
BLONDE ALE Colors: Light to medium yellow Flavors: Malt, Fruit, Hops	✓	✓		✓	✓		✓	✓
IPA Colors: Light yellow to red Flavors: Hops, Citrus, Pine	✓			✓	✓			✓
WHEAT BEERS Colors: Pale yellow to orange Flavors: Orange, Coriander, Banana	✓	✓		✓			✓	✓

heat is so high and the amount of alcohol so small (less than 1 tablespoon per serving), the amount of alcohol left behind is negligible.

Because of this, it's widely accepted that the consumption of cooked beer is safe for minors and pregnant women, although this is a personal decision that all beer-food consumers should make for themselves. Similarly, an important issue remains about the moral aspects of beer in food. If you are cooking for a person whose religion forbids the consumption of alcohol in all forms, then you have a moral obligation to disclose the fact that you are serving food cooked with beer. As well, the taste of beer may be intensely triggering to people who are recovering from alcohol addiction. Please disclose this information to anyone who you believe may have an issue with the consumption of alcohol. Because if you knowingly serve a beer-flavored dish to an alcoholic without letting him know what he is consuming, you are officially a jackass.

Although most of the recipes in this book are generally safe, I've added a code in the table of contents as a warning. Any time that the beer hasn't been cooked and large amounts of uncooked alcohol are present in the recipes, this symbol will appear: [H]. When small amounts of uncooked beer are present in one or more components, this symbol will appear: [M]. Please use your own well-considered judgment when serving beer-food to others.

Now that you have had your crash course in beer recipe development, please go cook your beer-loving hearts out. And don't forget to share.

Chapter 1

= BREAKFAST =

Amber Ale Pecan Cinnamon Rolls with
Beer Cream Cheese Frosting [M] . . . 26

Apple Cheddar Beer Pancakes . . . 28

Beer and Buttermilk Biscuits . . . 30

Chocolate Stout French Toast Casserole . . . 31

Chocolate Chip and Smoked Porter Pancakes . . . 33

Croque Madame with Beer Cheese Sauce . . . 34

Orange Wheat Beer and Dark Chocolate Muffins [M] . . . 36

Wheat Beer Dutch Babies . . . 37

Sausage and Pale Ale Frittata . . . 38

Pale Ale Corn Waffles with Scrambled Eggs and
Smoky Beer Cheese Sauce . . . 40

Amber Ale PECAN CINNAMON ROLLS WITH BEER CREAM CHEESE FROSTING [M]

8–12 CINNAMON ROLLS

|||||||||||||||||||||||||||||||||||||||||||||||||||||||||||||||||

FOR THE DOUGH:

3½ cups all-purpose flour
½ cup white sugar
1 packet rapid-rise yeast (do not use regular dry active yeast)
¼ cup dry milk powder
¼ cup unsalted butter
¼ cup cream
¾ cup amber ale
2 large egg yolks, room temperature
½ teaspoon salt

FOR THE FILLING:

½ cup unsalted butter, softened
½ cup white sugar
½ cup brown sugar
2 tablespoons cinnamon
½ cup chopped pecans

FOR THE FROSTING:

½ cup unsalted butter, softened
8 weight ounces cream cheese, softened
2 cups powdered sugar
¼ cup amber ale

Homemade cinnamon rolls are what you make when you really want to impress those breakfast guests. You can even start these ahead of time by letting the second rise take place over 12 hours in a refrigerator. Just allow the dough to come to room temperature prior to baking. The baked cinnamon rolls offer the alluring flavors of beer and a melt-in-your-mouth texture that will make you the most unforgettable breakfast host.

1. In the bowl of a stand mixer fitted with a dough hook add the flour, sugar, rapid rise yeast, and dry milk powder. Stir to combine.

2. In a microwave-safe bowl, melt the butter in the microwave. Add the cream and amber ale and microwave on high for 15 seconds. Test the temperature of the liquid with a cooking thermometer and repeat until it reaches 120°F–125°F.

3. Add liquid to the mixer and stir until incorporated.

4. Add the egg yolks and salt and mix on medium-high speed until dough comes together and gathers around the blade.

5. Place the dough in a lightly oiled large bowl (the oil will prevent the dough from sticking during the rise), cover with plastic wrap, and allow to sit in a warm room until doubled in size, 1½–2 hours.

6. On a lightly floured surface roll out the dough to an approximately 12" × 16" rectangle.

7. In a medium-sized bowl stir together the butter, sugars, and cinnamon.

8. Spread the cinnamon-sugar butter evenly over the dough; sprinkle with pecans. Starting at the long end, roll the dough into a tight log.

9. Cut the log into 2" rolls and place them cut side up in a 9" × 9" baking dish that has been sprayed with cooking spray. Cover with plastic wrap or a clean dish towel and allow dough to rise until doubled, about 45 minutes.

10. Heat oven to 350°F. Bake until golden brown, about 22–25 minutes. Remove from oven and allow to cool in the pan while the frosting is being assembled.

11. To make the frosting, beat the softened butter and cream cheese until fluffy. Add the powdered sugar and mix until well combined. Add the beer and continue mixing until light and fluffy. Spread frosting on warm rolls prior to serving.

Choose the Right Brew!

This is a recipe that needs the caramel flavors of an amber ale. Look for one with notes of caramel, cinnamon, or cloves. Stay away from beers that are too hop-forward.

Apple Cheddar BEER PANCAKES

12–14 PANCAKES

1¼ cups all-purpose flour
3 tablespoons sugar
1 tablespoon baking powder
1 teaspoon baking soda
1 teaspoon cinnamon
½ teaspoon salt
⅔ cup Cheddar
1 large Granny Smith apple, peeled and
   diced (about 1¼ cups)
⅔ cup Pilsner or blonde ale
⅓ cup buttermilk
3 tablespoons melted unsalted butter
1 large egg
2 tablespoons unsalted butter
   (plus additional if needed)

Apple and Cheddar are one of those improbable flavor combinations that most likely started with a dare and ended with an epic pairing. There is just something about the tang of Cheddar and the sweet acidity of apples that work so well together. Add in some beer and you have yourself some unforgettable pancakes.

1. Preheat an electric griddle to 350°F or a large skillet over medium-high heat.

2. In a large bowl combine the flour, sugar, baking powder, baking soda, cinnamon, and salt. Add the cheese and apples, and stir to combine.

3. In a separate bowl whisk together the beer, buttermilk, and melted butter. Add the egg and whisk to combine.

4. Make a well in the dry ingredients. Add the wet ingredients and stir until just combined.

5. Push the remaining 2 tablespoons butter around the griddle or skillet until melted.

6. Drop about ¼ cup of batter onto the buttered cooking surface. Cook until the underside has browned and the edges have started to dry, 2–4 minutes. Flip and allow to cook until cooked through, an additional 3–5 minutes. Serve warm with syrup.

Choose the Right Brew!

Grab a medium-hopped beer with notes of cloves and cinnamon for this recipe.
A pilsner or blonde ale will do fine, but for a more intense beer taste
look for a higher dose of hops.

BEER AND BUTTERMILK *Biscuits*

2 cups cake flour
1½ cups all-purpose flour
2 teaspoons baking powder
1½ teaspoons baking soda
1 teaspoon granulated sugar
1 teaspoon salt
8 tablespoons unsalted butter,
    cut into cubes
½ cup buttermilk
⅔ cup pale ale
2 tablespoons unsalted butter,
    melted
¼ teaspoon coarse sea salt

There really isn't anything quite like a warm homemade biscuit, right out of the oven. Beer adds a really nice texture and flavor that make this biscuit recipe one of a kind.

1. Preheat oven to 475°F.

2. In a large bowl combine the cake flour, all-purpose flour, baking powder, baking soda, sugar, and salt.

3. Add the butter cubes and rub into the flour using your fingers or a pastry cutter until butter is completely mixed into the flour.

4. Make a well in the dry ingredients and add the buttermilk and beer. Mix with a fork until just combined.

5. Add to a well-floured flat surface. Using a cold rolling pin (preferably marble), gently roll into a large rectangle, about ½" in thickness, using as few strokes as possible.

6. Fold the dough into thirds as you would a letter about to go into an envelope.

7. Using a biscuit cutter cut out 6-8 biscuits. Place in a 9" cake pan or 8" × 8" baking pan that has been sprayed with cooking spray.

8. Brush with melted butter and sprinkle with salt. Bake at 475°F for 9-11 minutes or until the tops are golden brown.

Choose the Right Brew!

A pale ale is the right man for this job. For a stronger punch of beer, look for one with a large hop presence; for a more mild beer taste, grab a lower-hop pale ale or even a wheat beer.

Chocolate Stout
FRENCH TOAST CASSEROLE

6–8 SERVINGS

|||||||||||||||||||||||||||||||||||||||||||||||||||||

1 loaf crusty French bread, cut into
 1" cubes (about 7 cups)
1½ cups whole milk
1 (4-weight ounce) bar of 60 percent
 dark chocolate, chopped (about
 ⅔ cup)
1 cup chocolate stout
6 large eggs
½ cup granulated sugar
½ cup brown sugar, packed

Is it bread pudding? Is it French toast? Who cares! It's delicious. Serve it topped with syrup and a side of bacon for breakfast or with whipped cream and a tall beer as a dessert. Either way it's a chocolate stout winner.

1. In a 9" × 13" baking dish arrange the bread cubes in an even layer.

2. In the top of a double boiler over medium-low heat (or a metal bowl set over but not touching simmering water), add the milk and the chocolate. Stir until chocolate has melted completely; remove from heat.

3. Add the stout and stir to combine. Cool to room temperature.

4. In a separate bowl, add eggs, granulated sugar, and brown sugar; whisk until well combined. Whisk the chocolate mixture into the egg mixture until well combined.

5. Pour over bread cubes, and toss lightly to coat.

6. Cover and refrigerate for 2–24 hours.

7. Heat oven to 325°F. Cook uncovered until set, about 45–55 minutes. Serve warm.

Choose the Right Brew!

Stouts and porters are fairly interchangeable when it comes to baking, so look for a dark beer with notes of cocoa, espresso, or even hints of smoke. Obviously, chocolate stout is your go-to for this recipe, but a smoked porter would be a fun twist.

CHOCOLATE CHIP AND SMOKED PORTER
Pancakes

MAKES 10 LARGE PANCAKES

1½ cups flour
¼ cup unsweetened cocoa powder
¼ teaspoon sea salt or kosher salt
1 tablespoon baking powder
¼ cup sugar
2 large eggs
¾ cup smoked porter beer
2 tablespoons melted butter
1 teaspoon vanilla
½ cup whole milk
¼ cup dark chocolate chips
1 tablespoon unsalted butter (plus
   additional if needed)

Putting beer in pancakes isn't just to make you feel like a breakfast rebel. The mild leavening powers of beer give your griddle cakes a nice lightness and great texture. But you can keep that part to yourself—you're having beer for breakfast!

1. Preheat electric griddle to 350°F, or a large skillet over medium-high heat.

2. In a large bowl combine flour, cocoa powder, salt, baking powder, and sugar.

3. In a separate bowl, whisk eggs and porter. Then add the melted butter, vanilla, and milk, whisking until combined.

4. Make a well in the dry ingredients, add the wet ingredients, and stir until just combined. Stir in the chocolate chips.

5. Add the remaining butter to the electric griddle (or skillet, heated on the stove top) and move butter around until melted.

6. Drop about ¼ cup of batter onto the buttered cooking surface. Cook until the underside has browned and the edges have started to dry, 2–4 minutes. Flip and allow to cook until cooked through, an additional 3–5 minutes.

7. Serve immediately.

Choose the Right Brew!

If you have never had a smoked porter, here is a great excuse to go find one. The flavors of smoke in these dark beers are a really good complement to the chocolate. If you can't get your hands on one, look for a stout or a porter with notes of chocolate.

Croque Madame
WITH BEER CHEESE SAUCE

SERVES 6

1 cup blonde ale
2 cups shredded white Cheddar
1 cup whole milk
2 tablespoons flour
2 tablespoons cornstarch
2 tablespoons unsalted butter
6 focaccia buns, or 6 (4") squares of focaccia bread
1 pound ham, sliced
7 weight ounces sliced Swiss cheese
6 large eggs

Choose the Right Brew!

A blonde ale will play nice, but if you want a real bold beer punch, up the hops and grab an IPA. It's up to you, but stick to the paler end of the scale for this one. Stouts and porters aren't allowed in this crowd.

A Croque Madame is a fancy name for a ham-and-cheese sandwich topped with an egg. Focaccia bread, homemade (foolproof) beer cheese sauce, and fresh-sliced ham will make this sandwich something to remember. Sandwiches can be made in a grill pan, the oven, or a panini press. Don't forget about this when you have half of a ham taunting you from the fridge (think: the day after Easter or Canadian Boxing Day).

1. Preheat oven to 375°F (if using, or preheat panini press or grill).
2. In a food processor or blender add the beer, white Cheddar, milk, flour, and cornstarch, and process until smooth, about 5 minutes.
3. In a pot over medium-high heat melt the butter. Add the cheese mixture and whisk continuously until thickened, then set aside.
4. Split focaccia buns, evenly divide ham between the buns, and top with 1–2 slices of Swiss cheese.
5. Arrange sandwiches on a baking sheet and bake at 375°F until cheese has melted, about 5 minutes.
6. Fry eggs until over medium heat in a skillet that has been sprayed with cooking spray, and remove from heat when the whites have set but the yolks are still runny.
7. Plate sandwiches and top with generous amounts of beer cheese sauce and a fried egg. Serve immediately.

Orange Wheat Beer
AND DARK CHOCOLATE MUFFINS [M]

MAKES 12–14 MUFFINS

Muffins are the way we eat cake for breakfast.

FOR THE MUFFINS:
1 large navel orange
½ cup granulated sugar
½ cup brown sugar
½ cup unsalted butter, softened
1 large egg
1 teaspoon vanilla extract
¼ cup buttermilk
⅔ cup wheat beer
2 cups cake flour
1 teaspoon baking powder
½ teaspoon baking soda
1 teaspoon salt
1 cup dark chocolate chips

FOR THE GLAZE:
1 cup confectioners' sugar
1 tablespoon wheat beer
1 teaspoon orange zest
1 tablespoon orange juice

1. Preheat oven to 375°F.

2. Zest the orange. Add 2 tablespoons zest to the bowl in a stand mixer, reserving 1 teaspoon zest for the glaze. Juice the orange; set juice aside.

3. Add the sugars and the softened butter to the zest in the stand mixer bowl. Mix on medium-high until well combined and fluffy.

4. Add the egg and vanilla, and beat on high until well combined, stopping to scrape the bottom of the bowl.

5. Add 2 tablespoons orange juice to the bowl. (Reserve 1 tablespoon orange juice for the glaze.) Mix on high until well combined.

6. Add the buttermilk and beer, and mix until combined.

7. In a separate bowl, stir together the flour, baking powder, baking soda, and salt. Stop the stand mixer and remove the bowl. Sprinkle the dry ingredients, as well as the chocolate chips, over the wet ingredients and stir gently with a wooden spoon until just combined.

8. Line 12-14 muffin cups with muffin papers. Divide batter evenly between the muffin cups. Place muffins in oven and reduce oven temperature to 325°F. Bake at 325°F for 22-27 minutes or until lightly golden brown.

9. To make the glaze whisk together confectioners' sugar, beer, zest, and reserved orange juice. Once muffins have cooled, glaze prior to serving.

Choose the Right Brew!

A wheat beer with notes of cloves, such as a hefeweizen or a Belgian white beer, is a great beer to grab for these muffins.

Wheat Beer DUTCH BABIES

SERVES 4

3 tablespoons unsalted butter, melted
⅔ cup wheat beer, room temperature
⅔ cup flour
3 large eggs, room temperature
¼ cup granulated sugar
1 teaspoon vanilla
1 cup fresh strawberries, chopped
⅔ cup confectioners' sugar
½ cup wheat beer

Dutch babies, or oven pancakes, are fairly easy but rather fickle. Allowing the batter to sit at room temperature for 10 minutes and placing the pan toward the bottom of the oven help generate a higher level of success with this puffy pancake.

1. Melt the butter in a 9" cast-iron skillet over medium-high heat. Remove pan from heat and swirl it to coat with butter.

2. In a food processor or blender add the beer, flour, eggs, sugar, and vanilla. Process until well blended. Add the butter and then process until combined.

3. Add the batter to the cast-iron skillet and allow it to sit at room temperature for 10 minutes prior to baking.

4. Place the oven rack at the lowest position. Preheat oven to 450°F.

5. Place the cast-iron skillet in the oven and bake at 450°F for 18–22 minutes or until Dutch Babies are light golden brown and slightly puffed.

6. Cut into 4 equal slices, top with strawberries, and dust with confectioners' sugar. Serve immediately.

Choose the Right Brew!

A good white ale or hefeweizen will give a nice citrusy bready taste to these oven pancakes. Look for a wheat beer with a higher hop profile for a larger beer taste.

SAUSAGE AND PALE ALE *Frittata*

SERVES 4–6

8 large eggs

1 medium jalapeño, chopped and seeded (about ¼ cup)

⅓ cup Parmesan cheese

3 basil leaves, chopped into thin ribbons

½ teaspoon salt

½ teaspoon pepper

¼ cup pale ale, plus ½ cup, divided

1 tablespoon milk

2 tablespoons unsalted butter

½ French or sour dough baguette, cut into 1" cubes (about 2 cups)

2 tablespoons vegetable oil

1 red bell pepper, chopped

2 links raw sweet Italian sausage, removed from casing, crumbled (8 weight ounces total)

Who says you can't have beer for breakfast? Deglazing the pan with beer after the sausage has begun to cook brings out some of those great flavors that might otherwise be lost in the depths of the skillet. And it gives you a legitimate reason to open a beer before noon.

1. Preheat oven to 375°F.

2. In a large bowl, add the eggs, jalapeño, Parmesan cheese, basil, salt, pepper, ¼ cup beer, and milk and whisk until well combined. Set aside.

3. In a 10" cast-iron skillet melt the butter over medium-high heat.

4. Add the bread; toss to coat. Cook until lightly golden brown; remove from pan.

5. Add the oil to the pan and allow the oil to get hot but not smoking. Add the bell peppers and sausage; cook until sausage has started to brown. Add the remaining ½ cup beer and stir.

6. Add the bread back into the pan and arrange it in an even layer.

7. Add the egg mixture and allow it to cook until the sides have set, about 3–5 minutes.

8. Transfer skillet to the oven and cook until the middle has set, about 16–20 minutes.

9. Serve immediately.

Choose the Right Brew!

A pale ale is a great way to go with this. The beer flavor is rather mild, and a kick of hops will help it come through. Pick a beer that has some citrus—some notes of basil or other herbs would also work well.

Pale Ale CORN WAFFLES WITH SCRAMBLED EGGS AND SMOKY BEER CHEESE SAUCE

SERVES 6

FOR THE WAFFLES:
1 cup fine-ground yellow cornmeal
1½ cups all-purpose flour
1 teaspoon baking powder
½ teaspoon salt
¼ cup Cheddar cheese, shredded
   (do not use preshredded)
¼ cup brown sugar
¼ teaspoon chili powder
1 cup corn kernels (thawed if frozen)
½ cup melted unsalted butter
½ cup buttermilk
⅔ cup wheat beer
1 tablespoon canola oil
2 large eggs, separated

This is a perfect brunch recipe that will keep you full all morning. A savory waffle, soft scrambled eggs, and some creamy beer cheese sauce will surely be a crowd pleaser.

1. Heat waffle iron to manufacturer's specifications.

2. To make the waffles, set out three large bowls. In one bowl, add the cornmeal, flour, baking powder, salt, Cheddar cheese, brown sugar, chili powder, and corn kernels.

3. In another bowl, whisk together the melted butter, buttermilk, beer, and oil. Whisk in the egg yolks.

4. In a third bowl, add the egg whites and beat on high with a hand mixer until light and frothy, about 3 minutes.

5. Add the beer mixture to the flour mixture and stir until just combined. Gently fold in the egg whites.

6. Cook waffles in waffle iron according to manufacturer's specifications.

7. To make the cheese sauce, add the flour, cornstarch, beer, Gouda, Cheddar, smoked paprika, and milk to a blender or food processor. Process on high until very well blended, 5–8 minutes.

FOR THE CHEESE SAUCE:

2 tablespoons flour
1 tablespoon cornstarch
1 cup wheat beer
1 cup freshly shredded smoked Gouda
   (do not use preshredded)
1 cup freshly shredded Cheddar
   (do not use preshredded)
¼ teaspoon smoked paprika
1 cup whole milk
2 tablespoons unsalted butter

FOR THE EGGS:

12 large eggs
¼ cup whole milk
½ teaspoon salt
½ teaspoon pepper
1 tablespoon unsalted butter

8. Melt the butter over medium heat and add the cheese mixture, cooking until thickened, stirring continuously, 5–8 minutes. If small bits of cheese solids remain, blend until smooth with a hand blender.

9. To make the eggs, in a large bowl add the eggs, milk, salt, and pepper, and whisk until very well combined. Melt butter in a skillet over medium heat, add eggs, and cook until the bottom starts to set, about 1 minute.

10. Gently pull the eggs from the edges into the center with a wooden spoon. Repeat until the eggs are still slightly soft; they will continue to set as they cool. Remove from heat.

11. Plate the waffle. Top with eggs and sauce. Serve immediately.

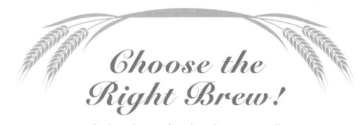

Choose the Right Brew!

The breadiness of a wheat beer goes well with this recipe, and the traditional low-hop profile of a hefeweizen or a Belgium white won't overwhelm an early morning palate.

Chapter 2

APPETIZERS, STARTERS, and SIDES

Baked Brie with Amber Ale–Caramelized Apples and Pancetta . . . 44

Beer-Braised Green Beans with Bacon and Shallots . . . 46

Beer Grits with Goat Cheese and Chives . . . 47

Beer Cheese Gratin Potatoes . . . 49

Chili Con Queso Cerveza Crostini . . . 50

IPA Guacamole [M] . . . 51

Jalapeños and Bacon Beer Cheese Dip . . . 52

Roasted Garlic IPA Hummus [H] . . . 53

Porter Caramelized Onion Dip [M] . . . 54

Roasted Garlic Pale Ale Whipped Potatoes [H] . . . 56

Soft Pretzels with Chipotle Beer
Cheese Sauce . . . 57

Baked Brie WITH AMBER ALE–CARAMELIZED APPLES AND PANCETTA

1 WHEEL OF BAKED BRIE

1 large Honeycrisp apple, peeled, cored, and diced (can substitute Fuji or Granny Smith apples)
¼ cup unsalted butter
½ cup amber ale
⅓ cup brown sugar
½ cup diced pancetta
1 sheet puff pastry or single pie crust
8 weight ounces (small wheel) soft ripened brie

Creamy baked brie with caramelized apples and pancetta, with a kick of beer, oozing inside a flaky crust! This will make you an entertaining superhero. You may even make some craft beer converts with this one.

1. Preheat oven to 400°F.
2. In a pan over medium-high heat add the apples, butter, beer, and brown sugar. Cook, stirring occasionally, until the apples are soft and the beer has reduced to a syrupy consistency, about 10 minutes.
3. In a separate skillet, cook the pancetta over medium-high heat until slightly crispy, about 5 minutes.
4. Roll the pastry out on a lightly floured surface until large enough to fit over the brie. Transfer pastry to a baking sheet that has been sprayed with cooking spray. Place the brie in the center of the pastry, top with the apples, then add the pancetta. Fold the pastry up over the brie, pressing together to secure tightly.
5. Bake at 400°F for 25–30 minutes or until pastry has started to brown. Serve warm on a platter with crackers or toast points.

Choose the Right Brew!

The caramel flavors will work best with a beer with caramel notes. Reach for an amber ale and those flavors will come through. Because the beer will be reduced, the hops will be intensified. Look for a low-hop beer to avoid any unappetizing bitterness.

Beer-Braised Green Beans
WITH BACON AND SHALLOTS

6 SERVINGS

3 strips thick-sliced bacon
1 medium shallot, minced (about ¼ cup)
4 cups fresh green beans, trimmed and cut in half
1 cup pale ale
1 cup breadcrumbs
¼ teaspoon smoked paprika
½ teaspoon black pepper
½ teaspoon salt
1 large egg white
1 tablespoon water
1 large shallot, cut into ⅛" rings

Choose the Right Brew!

Look for a medium-hopped pale ale, or even a slightly higher–hopped wheat beer. A large dose of hops will give you a strong beer taste, if that's what you're looking for. A mild wheat beer or pale ale will give you just a touch of that brewed flavor.

Move over, green bean casserole packed with canned beans! This is a grown–up version, complete with oven–crisped shallots, beer–caramelized bacon, and a boozy finish. Thanksgiving will never be the same once you beerify the sides.

1. Preheat oven to 375°F.

2. In a large skillet, cook the bacon over medium-high heat until most of the fat has rendered but the bacon isn't yet crispy. Remove the bacon from the pan. Pour off about half of the bacon fat, leaving about 2 tablespoons in the pan. Chop the bacon.

3. Add the minced shallots and green beans and cook in the bacon fat for 3 minutes.

4. Pour the beer over the green beans, stirring the bottom of the pan to loosen any brown bits. Add the chopped bacon back to the pan. Lower heat and simmer, stirring occasionally, until the beer is mostly gone, about 10 minutes.

5. While the green beans are cooking, work on the shallot rings. In a medium-sized bowl combine the breadcrumbs, smoked paprika, black pepper, and salt.

6. In a separate bowl, beat the egg white with 1 tablespoon water. Add the shallot rings, and stir until well coated. Remove the shallot rings from the egg whites and add to the breadcrumbs. Toss to coat.

7. Pour the breadcrumbs and the shallots onto a baking sheet, spreading them out evenly. Place in the oven and bake at 375°F until breadcrumbs are golden brown and shallots are softened, about 10–15 minutes.

8. Add green beans to a serving dish. Top with shallot rings and breadcrumbs.

Beer Grits WITH
GOAT CHEESE AND CHIVES

4–6 SERVINGS

1 cup pale ale beer
1½ cups whole milk
1 cup heavy cream
Pinch salt
1 cup corn grits
4 tablespoons unsalted butter
Salt and pepper to taste
3 weight ounces goat cheese, crumbled
¼ cup chives, chopped

Grits are a Southern standard, and I do hope the South forgives me for what I've done to them. With an infusion of beer and a creamy goat cheese finish, it's a side dish that will get people talking.

1. Add beer, milk, cream, and a pinch of salt to a large pot over medium heat and bring to a gentle simmer. Slowly whisk in the grits.

2. Simmer, stirring occasionally, until tender, about 20 minutes. Adjust the heat to maintain a simmer.

3. Whisk in the butter, stirring until completely combined. Salt and pepper to taste.

4. Pour into serving bowls, top with goat cheese and chives, and serve immediately.

Choose the Right Brew!

A pale ale will work great in this recipe, but so will a brown ale. Look for low- to medium-hopped beer with warm notes of nuts or cloves to give a mellow beer flavor to this creamy bowl of grits.

Beer Cheese GRATIN POTATOES

6 SERVINGS

IIIIIIIIIIIIIIIIIIIIIIIIIIIIIIIIIIIIIIIIIIIIIIIIIIIIIIIIII

1 cup pale ale
1 cup freshly shredded Gruyère cheese, plus ½ cup (do not use preshredded)
1 cup freshly shredded white Cheddar, plus ½ cup (do not use preshredded)
1 cup whole milk
2 tablespoons flour
1 tablespoon cornstarch
2 tablespoons unsalted butter
½ teaspoon salt
1 teaspoon pepper
½ teaspoon garlic powder
4 cups red potatoes, peeled and thinly sliced
¾ cup panko breadcrumbs

This is what your great–grandmother would have served at Thanksgiving if she had been a brewmaster: a classic cheesy potato dish, infused with the great flavors of craft beer. This is a side dish that means business.

1. In a food processor add the beer, 1 cup Gruyère cheese, 1 cup Cheddar, whole milk, flour, and cornstarch. Process until smooth, about 5 minutes.

2. In a large pan or pot, melt the butter over medium-high heat. Add the cheese mixture and whisk continually until slightly thickened, about 3 minutes. Stir in the salt, pepper, and garlic powder.

3. Add the potatoes to the cheese sauce. Simmer until the potatoes have softened slightly but aren't yet fork tender, 12–15 minutes.

4. Pour potato cheese mixture into a 2-quart baking dish, arranging into a fairly even layer.

5. Sprinkle with remaining shredded cheese. Sprinkle with panko.

6. Bake at 375°F until panko has browned and the potatoes are tender, 30–40 minutes. If panko starts to brown before potatoes are tender, cover with foil and continue to bake.

Choose the Right Brew!

This recipe is a Choose Your Own Adventure, Hops Edition. The higher-hopped beer you use, the more prominent the beer flavor. If you want a beer punch to the mouth, pick an IPA. If you want a mellow flavor, reach for a wheat beer or a lower-hop pale ale, pilsner, or blonde ale.

CHILI CON QUESO *Cerveza Crostini*

20–24 CROSTINIS

1 tablespoon unsalted butter
1 jalapeño, stemmed, seeded, and chopped
1 poblano, stemmed seeded and chopped
1 cup shredded sharp Cheddar
1 cup shredded jack cheese
⅔ cup IPA
8 weight ounces cream cheese
3 tablespoons cornstarch
2 French baguettes, cut into ½" slices
⅓ cup cilantro, minced
2 firm Roma tomatoes, diced
2 large avocados, sliced

This idea was born out of necessity. I noticed that during parties people congregated near the dip; no one ever loaded up a party plate with dip and moved away from the table. To solve this dilemma, I started spreading the beer cheese dip on tiny portable rounds of bread. Now people fill up plates and move on, and party mingling is much more harmonious.

1. Preheat broiler.

2. In a pan over medium-high heat, melt the butter. Add both types of chopped peppers and cook until softened, stirring occasionally.

3. In a food processor add the Cheddar, jack cheese, beer, cream cheese, and cornstarch. Purée until smooth, about 5 minutes. Add to the pan with the peppers, stirring constantly until thickened, 6–8 minutes.

4. Arrange baguette slices on a baking sheet. Place under broiler until lightly browned, 1–2 minutes. Flip each slice and brown on the opposite side under broiler for an additional 1–2 minutes.

5. Spread each toasted baguette slice with a generous amount of the dip. Sprinkle with cilantro; top with tomato and avocado. Serve immediately.

Choose the Right Brew!

An IPA will give you a strong beer bite and compete with the strong pepper and cheese flavors in this appetizer. Look for a floral or citrusy high-hop beer.

IPA *Guacamole* [M]

4 CUPS

3 cups avocado flesh (about 4 large
    avocados)
1 tablespoon freshly squeezed lime
    juice
½ teaspoon chili powder
½ teaspoon garlic powder
¼ cup IPA beer
½ cup red onion, chopped
⅓ cup diced tomatoes
½ teaspoon salt
3 tablespoons cilantro, chopped
1 jalapeño, stemmed, seeded, and
    chopped (about 2½ tablespoons)

Adding some beer flavor to your next fiesta just got easier. Grab your favorite high-hop beer and make sure to enjoy this with chips, loud music, and lots of friends.

Add all ingredients to a bowl; mash. Serve with chips.

Choose the Right Brew!

This is a great recipe for a double-hopped IPA. Because a small amount of beer is called for, you need one that packs a punch — the more hops the better.

JALAPEÑOS AND BACON
Beer Cheese Dip

2½ CUPS

16 weight ounces cream cheese
1½ cups mozzarella
2 tablespoons cornstarch
½ cup pale ale
¼ teaspoon salt
½ teaspoon black pepper
1 teaspoon garlic powder
5 strips thick-sliced bacon, cooked and chopped
2 large jalapeños, stemmed, seeded, and chopped
Chips for serving

Sure, this is great right out of the pot, and your friends might end up licking the bowl if you run out of chips, but there are so many other ways to use this. Make crostinis by spreading it on toasted slices of baguette, make mini tarts with golden rounds of baked puff pastry, or use it as a spread to turn a chicken burger into The Best Chicken Burger of All Time.

1. In a food processor add the cream cheese, mozzarella, cornstarch, beer, salt, pepper, and garlic powder. Process until smooth, about 3 minutes.

2. Transfer to a pot over medium-high heat, stirring until warmed and just starting to bubble, about 5 minutes.

3. Turn off heat and stir in most of the bacon and jalapeños, reserving 2 tablespoons bacon and 1 tablespoon jalapeños for garnish.

4. Pour dip into a serving bowl, sprinkle with reserved bacon and jalapeños, and serve warm with chips.

Choose the Right Brew!

This is a dip for the paler end of the beer spectrum. Look for a medium-hopped pale ale with notes of citrus to set off the flavors in this spicy and smoky dip.

Roasted Garlic IPA HUMMUS [H]

2½ CUPS

1 head garlic
1 tablespoon olive oil
1 (15-weight ounce) can chickpeas,
   drained
⅓ cup IPA
2 tablespoons tahini
¼ teaspoon salt
1 tablespoon lemon juice
½ teaspoon onion powder
Pinch chili powder
Crudités, chips, or pita bread cut into
   quarters

Choose the Right Brew!

This is a great way to use an IPA. Since a relatively small amount of beer is used, the higher-hopped beers will give you the beer punch you are looking for and add some balance to the warmth of the roasted garlic. If you want a mellower beer flavor, look for a pale ale with lower hops.

Did you know that the thin transparent skin on chickpeas is what has always prevented you from getting a smooth and creamy homemade hummus? It may seem like a pain to stand at your sink for 15 minutes shelling chickpeas, but I promise you it's well worth it. You can even keep the secret to yourself when your guests are amazed that you made such a silky hummus—maybe you are just that good.

1. Preheat oven to 425°F.

2. Cut the pointed tip off the head of garlic, exposing the cloves. Place the garlic head on a small sheet of aluminum foil. Drizzle with olive oil and fold into a tight packet. Place garlic packet in a baking dish and roast at 425°F for 25–30 minutes, or until soft and the cloves have turned an amber color.

3. Place chickpeas in a small bowl; cover with cold water. One at a time, pinch the chickpeas gently to remove the thin transparent skin. Reserve chickpeas, discard skin.

4. Place skinned chickpeas in a food processor along with the IPA, tahini, salt, lemon juice, onion powder, and chili powder. Once the garlic has cooled enough to handle, gently squeeze the head until the soft cloves protrude. Add just the cloves to the food processor; discard the rest of the head. Process until smooth.

5. For a smoother texture, add additional beer or olive oil until desired texture is reached. Serve at room temperature with crudités, chips, or pita bread.

Porter CARAMELIZED ONION DIP [M]

3 CUPS

2 tablespoons unsalted butter

2 tablespoons oil

2 large sweet white onions, chopped

½ teaspoon salt

¼ cup porter, plus 3 tablespoons, divided

8 weight ounces cream cheese

1 cup sour cream

½ teaspoon black pepper

¼ teaspoon smoked paprika

½ teaspoon garlic powder

¼ cup green onions, chopped

Beer dip has never been so sophisticated. Creamy and smooth with the warm flavors of caramelized onions and porter, this is one dip your guests won't soon forget. It can also be spread on toasted baguette slices and topped with chives for an easy crostini. Don't be afraid to make this a few days ahead of time. The flavors deepen and intensify after it's been resting in the refrigerator for a day or two.

1. In a pan over medium heat, add the butter and oil. Stir until butter has melted.

2. Add the onions. Reduce heat to medium-low and cook until onions have started to soften, about 5 minutes.

3. Add the salt and ¼ cup porter and continue to cook, stirring occasionally, until the onions have caramelized, about 25 minutes. Do not cook on too high heat or the onions will burn rather than caramelize.

4. Add cream cheese, sour cream, caramelized onions, pepper, remaining porter, smoked paprika, and garlic powder to a food processor. Process until smooth. Add green onions; pulse once or twice to combine.

5. Serve warm.

Choose the Right Brew!

This dip screams for a porter with notes of smoke or even bourbon. Look for something bold, with warm notes to bring the flavors together.

Roasted Garlic
PALE ALE WHIPPED POTATOES [H]

4 CUPS

1 head garlic
1 tablespoon olive oil
2½ pounds red potatoes, peeled and
  chopped into quarters
¾ cup IPA beer
12 tablespoons unsalted butter
½ cup sour cream
1 teaspoon salt
1 teaspoon pepper

You can keep your smashed potatoes. I like mine whipped. The creamy texture reminds me of childhood Thanksgiving and Grandma's table. Of course, this visit to America's Favorite Side Dish has a kick of hops.

1. Preheat oven to 425°F.

2. Cut the pointed tip off the head of garlic, exposing the cloves. Place the garlic head on a small sheet of aluminum foil. Drizzle with olive oil and fold into a tight packet. Place garlic packet in a baking dish and roast at 425°F for 25–30 minutes, or until soft and the cloves have turned an amber color.

3. Add potatoes to a pot and cover with cold water and pinch of salt. Bring to a boil over medium-high heat. Cook until fork tender, 15–20 minutes after water begins to boil, drain.

4. Add potatoes and remaining ingredients to a stand mixer. Squeeze the head of garlic until the soft cloves push out. Add just the cloves to the stand mixer; discard the remaining head.

5. Whip the potatoes on high until well combined. Add additional salt and pepper to taste.

Choose the Right Brew!

Look for a pale ale with notes of nuts and herbs for this one. Just keep this in mind: The higher the hops, the stronger the beer flavor will be.

SOFT PRETZELS WITH CHIPOTLE
Beer Cheese Sauce

**MAKES 6 PRETZELS OR
ABOUT 48 PRETZEL BITES**

FOR PRETZEL:
2½ cups flour
1 tablespoon sugar
1 envelope rapid-rise yeast (do not use
   regular dry active yeast)
1 cup wheat beer
1 teaspoon kosher salt
2 tablespoons olive oil
10 cups water
½ cup baking soda
3 tablespoons melted unsalted butter
2 tablespoons coarse salt

FOR SAUCE:
½ cup wheat beer
1½ cups sharp Cheddar
½ cup milk
1 chipotle pepper in adobo
2 tablespoons cornstarch
2 tablespoons butter

Beer and pretzels have a long-standing romance. Here they team up in a beer-infused pretzel with a creamy, smoky, spicy beer cheese sauce for your dipping pleasure. Dough can either be made into 6 soft pretzels or about 48 pretzel bites.

1. In the bowl of a stand mixer fitted with a dough hook, add the flour, sugar, and yeast; mix on medium-low speed to combine.

2. In a microwave-safe dish, add the wheat beer. Microwave for 20 seconds, test temperature with a cooking thermometer, and repeat until beer reaches between 120°F and 125°F.

3. Add beer to the stand mixer and mix on medium speed until the flour has mostly been incorporated (stop to stir with a wooden spoon if necessary).

4. Add the salt and oil. Mix on high until the dough starts to gather around the blade, about 5 minutes.

5. Transfer dough to a bowl that has been lightly oiled with vegetable oil. Cover tightly with plastic wrap, and allow to sit in a warm room until doubled in size, 45–60 minutes.

6. Preheat oven to 425°F.

7. To make pretzels: Cut dough into 6 equal-sized pieces. Roll each dough piece into a 20"–22" rope. Form into a "U" shape and cross the ends over to form a pretzel shape. To make pretzel bites: Cut dough into 44–48 equal-sized pieces.

(continued)

8. Place pretzels or pretzel bites on a baking sheet covered with parchment paper or a silicone baking mat.

9. Place 10 cups of water in a large, wide pot. Make sure the pot is large enough that the water doesn't reach more than two-thirds of the way up the pot. Bring to a boil over high heat and then add the baking soda.

10. One at a time, add the pretzels to the boiling water (if making pretzel bites, add about 5 at a time). Allow pretzels to boil for about 30 seconds. Remove with a flat wide spatula, and return to the baking sheet. Brush with melted butter and sprinkle with coarse salt.

11. Bake at 425°F for 12–14 minutes, or until a dark golden brown.

12. To make the sauce, add the beer, cheese, milk, chipotle, and cornstarch to a blender or food processor. Blend on high for 3–5 minutes or until very well blended. In a pot over medium-high heat, melt the butter. Add the cheese mixture and stir continually until thickened, 8–10 minutes. Serve pretzels warm with warm cheese sauce on the side.

Choose the Right Brew!

Wheat beer pulls double duty for this one! Look for a wheat beer with lots of bready and malty notes and a medium-hop profile to give you the right kick. Remember that alcohol intensifies heat, so the higher the ABV of the beer used in the sauce, the spicier it will be.

Chapter 3

= SAUCES =

Amber Ale Caramel Sauce . . . 62

Chocolate Stout Fudge Sauce [H] . . . 63

Creamy Pale Ale Basil Pesto Sauce [M] . . . 64

Foolproof Beer Cheese Sauce . . . 65

IPA Puttanesca Sauce [M] . . . 66

IPA Honey Mustard Vinaigrette [H] . . . 69

Orange Hefeweizen Marmalade . . . 71

Maple Stout Barbecue Sauce . . . 73

Porter Fig Jam . . . 74

Stout-Balsamic Glaze . . . 75

Amber Ale
CARAMEL SAUCE

1½ CUPS

1 cup sugar
½ cup amber ale, plus 2 tablespoons, divided
2 tablespoons heavy cream
2 tablespoons unsalted butter, cut into cubes
½ teaspoon vanilla

Homemade caramel sauce sounds like quite the feat of culinary ingenuity, but it's actually very simple. Keep this in mind for homemade Christmas gifts or just The Best Ice Cream Social Ever.

1. In a saucepan over high heat, add the sugar and ½ cup amber ale.

2. Stir just until the sugar has dissolved. Allow to boil, occasionally swirling the pan (just don't stir), until the sauce is a dark amber color, 9–12 minutes.

3. Remove from heat and add cream, stirring constantly until combined.

4. Return to low heat. Add butter, vanilla, and remaining 2 tablespoons beer, stirring until well combined and smooth.

5. Remove from heat; allow to cool. Store in the refrigerator in an airtight container.

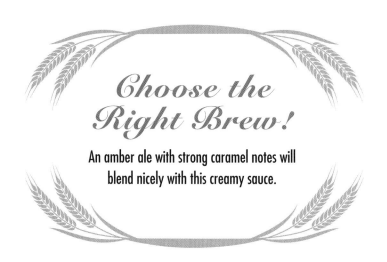

Choose the Right Brew!

An amber ale with strong caramel notes will blend nicely with this creamy sauce.

Chocolate Stout
FUDGE SAUCE [H]

2 CUPS

⅔ cup granulated sugar
⅔ cup unsweetened cocoa powder
¾ cup chocolate stout
3 weight ounces unsweetened bakers' chocolate
3 tablespoons unsalted butter
½ cup light corn syrup

The uses for a chocolate sauce made with a rich stout are endless. Use it for dipping fruit, pour it on ice cream, spread it between cookies, or drizzle it on your morning pancakes.

1. In a large bowl stir together the sugar and cocoa powder.

2. Whisk the stout into the dry ingredients; set aside.

3. In the top of a double boiler (or a metal bowl set over but not touching simmering water) melt the bakers' chocolate and butter, stirring frequently.

4. Add the melted chocolate and butter to the first bowl and whisk until well combined.

5. Add the corn syrup and stir until combined.

6. Use immediately or store in an airtight container in the refrigerator.

Choose the Right Brew!

For the right silky-smooth beer flavor, look for a chocolate stout that's been made with genuine cocoa, not an extract. A smoked porter with notes of chocolate or espresso would be an excellent choice as well.

Creamy Pale Ale
BASIL PESTO SAUCE [M]

1½ CUPS

2 cups fresh basil leaves, packed
¼ cup pine nuts
1 clove garlic
¼ cup olive oil
¼ cup IPA
¼ cup freshly shaved Parmesan
½ teaspoon white sugar
½ teaspoon black pepper
1 tablespoon unsalted butter
½ cup heavy cream

Creamy pesto is a quick and easy sauce to whip up from scratch—and so impressive. Toss it with your favorite cooked pasta or spread it on sandwiches for a welcome break from the mayo.

1. Add basil leaves, pine nuts, and garlic to a food processor. Process until mostly combined, about 2 minutes. While food processor is still running, slowly add the olive oil, then the beer. Add the Parmesan, sugar, and black pepper; pulse until well combined.

2. In a saucepan over medium-high heat, melt the butter. Add the heavy cream and the basil sauce. Stir until bubbly and slightly thickened, about 3 minutes. Serve over pasta. To use as a sandwich spread, chill prior to use.

Choose the Right Brew!

A strong citrusy IPA will pack the punch you need to compete with the strong basil and Parmesan flavors of this dish.

Foolproof
BEER CHEESE SAUCE

3 CUPS

1 cup freshly shredded Gouda (do not use preshredded)
1 cup freshly shredded Cheddar (do not use preshredded)
1 cup whole milk
2 tablespoons flour
1 tablespoon cornstarch
1 cup pale ale
2 tablespoons unsalted butter
Salt and pepper

If you have ever tried to make beer cheese sauce and failed, you aren't alone. The patience it takes to get a truly creamy, nonclumpy sauce is a skill set many people do not possess. I've fixed the issue, by way of the blender, to give you perfectly creamy sauce every time, in half the time.

1. Add Gouda, Cheddar, milk, flour, cornstarch, and beer to a blender or food processor. Process on high until very well blended, 5–8 minutes.

2. In a saucepan over medium-high heat, melt the butter. Add the sauce from the food processor and whisk rapidly and continuously until thickened, about 5 minutes.

3. Salt and pepper to taste. If small bits of cheese solids remain, blend until smooth with a hand blender. Serve warm.

Choose the Right Brew!

This is a sauce for a paler beer. Look for an American pale ale or a pilsner, with notes of spice or citrus. You can also use a wheat beer for a milder beer flavor, or if you want to ramp up the beer taste, reach for an IPA.

IPA
Puttanesca Sauce [M]

MAKES 5 CUPS

|||||||||||||||||||||||||||||||||||||||||||||||||||||||||||||||||||||

1 head garlic
1 tablespoon olive oil, plus 2 tablespoons divided
2 pounds heirloom or beefsteak tomatoes, quartered (about 6–8 large)
6 mini sweet peppers, stemmed and quartered
1 teaspoon salt
2 large leaves basil, chopped (about 2 tablespoons)
8 Kalamata olives, pitted
1 teaspoon red pepper flakes
2 tablespoons balsamic glaze
⅓ cup IPA beer
½ teaspoon black pepper
1 tablespoon capers
Cooked pasta for serving

How about a vegan pasta sauce that can be made in advance and that's hearty enough to satisfy your carnivorous friends? Thanks to roasted veggies and a punch of IPA, you'll never miss the meat.

1. Cut the pointed tip off the head of garlic, exposing the cloves. Place the garlic head on a small sheet of aluminum foil. Drizzle with olive oil and fold into a tight packet. Place garlic packet on a baking sheet.

2. Add the tomatoes and sweet peppers to the baking sheet; drizzle with remaining 2 tablespoons olive oil. Toss tomatoes and peppers until well coated with olive oil; sprinkle with salt.

3. Roast at 425°F for 20–25 minutes. Remove from oven and allow to cool enough to handle. The skin of the tomatoes should easily peel away. Peel off tomato skins and discard.

4. Place the tomato flesh in a large food processor or blender along with the roasted sweet peppers and any juices in the baking pan.

5. Remove garlic from foil packet and squeeze the head until the soft cloves emerge. Add the cloves to the food processor, discard the remaining head.

(continued)

6. Add the remaining ingredients and process until smooth, 3–5 minutes. (Sauce can also be puréed in a large pot with an immersion blender.)

7. Store in an airtight container until ready to use. To heat, add to a pot over medium-high heat; stir until warmed. Serve over pasta.

Choose the Right Brew!

This is a great recipe for an IPA. The bold flavors of a high-hop beer can hold their own against the hearty flavors in this sauce.

Note: Mini sweet peppers are related to the bell pepper but are smaller and sweeter. Look for them in the produce section; they are usually sold in 1-pound packages with yellow, red, and orange peppers combined. You can make balsamic glaze by reducing balsamic and a pinch of sugar until thick and syrupy, or you can find prepared balsamic glaze in the vinegar section near the balsamic vinegar.

IPA HONEY MUSTARD
Vinaigrette [H]

MAKES 1¼ CUPS

⅓ cup Dijon mustard
3 tablespoons honey
½ cup IPA
¼ cup shallots, chopped
2 cloves garlic, smashed
½ teaspoon black pepper
2 tablespoons lemon juice

Vinaigrettes are a great sauce to make from scratch. The complementary flavors of honey and mustard go well with a dose of high hops. This is quick and easy and comes together in just a few minutes.

1. Add all ingredients to a food processor; process until smooth.

2. Store in an airtight container in the refrigerator.

Choose the Right Brew!

A high-hop beer with notes of citrus is a great choice for this sauce.

ORANGE HEFEWEIZEN
Marmalade

3 CUPS

1 pound seedless navel oranges
   (about 2 large)
1 tablespoon whole cloves
4½ cups sugar
24 fluid ounces hefeweizen
2 tablespoons lemon juice

A high tea is such a fancy place to find some beer. This isn't just for crumpets and muffins; it can be used on your morning waffles or beer-and-buttermilk biscuits, and it can also be used in an orange chili chicken marinade.

1. Cut oranges into quarters. Very thinly slice each orange quarter. (Make sure no seeds remain; seeds will make the marmalade very bitter.)

2. Place cloves on a small piece of cheesecloth and tie tightly with kitchen twine. (An empty loose leaf tea bag, tied tightly, can be used instead.)

3. Place oranges, clove packet, sugar, and beer in a very large stockpot. Bring to a simmer, stirring frequently, and allow to simmer for 5 minutes (do not boil). Turn off heat. Cover pot with lid and allow to sit at room temperature overnight.

4. Uncover, remove and discard clove packet, and bring back to a simmer over medium-low heat. Reduce heat to maintain a very low simmer over low heat for 2 hours. As it simmers, skim off any white film that gathers at the top.

5. After 2 hours, add lemon juice and clip a candy thermometer onto the pot. Bring mixture to a medium simmer over medium heat. Simmer gently between 180°F and 200°F for 20–30 minutes, then turn off heat. Using a pair of tongs, remove about half of the orange rinds, focusing on removing the larger rinds and leaving the smaller slices. (Leaving all of the oranges in the marmalade is fine, if desired.)

(continued)

6. Turn heat on high, bring mixture to 220°F, and remove from heat. Marmalade will thicken as it cools. To check the doneness of the marmalade, put a dime-sized amount on a plate and chill it for 10 minutes. If the marmalade is still runny, return it to a boil until thickened. If it's too thick, add a bit of water. Can if desired, or store in an airtight container in the refrigerator until ready to use, up to a week.

Choose the Right Brew!

Look for a citrusy wheat beer, and even one that has been made with the goodness of oranges. A beer with a low- to medium-hop profile and notes of cloves will do just fine as well.

Note: To candy the orange slices that are removed from the marmalade, lay them flat on a baking sheet that has been covered with a silicone baking mat or parchment paper that has been sprayed with cooking spray, and bake at 200°F for about 1 hour.

Maple Stout BARBECUE SAUCE

2 CUPS

1 tablespoon olive oil
1 shallot, minced
4 cloves garlic, minced
1 cup stout beer
½ cup low-sodium soy sauce
⅔ cup ketchup
2 tablespoons Worcestershire sauce
1 teaspoon hot red chili sauce
2 teaspoons smoked paprika
⅓ cup real maple syrup
1 teaspoon onion powder

America runs on barbecue. It's in our blood, and it provides a common thread that runs through our childhood summers. Whether you grill your food, use a proper low and slow barbecue, or just have a bunch of friends over for some burgers and slap a "Barbecue" label on the day, it's part of our culture. To keep the tradition rolling, a terrific homemade barbecue sauce makes the perfect addition to any home cook's culinary repertoire. The meat–tenderizing properties of beer is a great jumping–off point. Add a little heat, balance it with the sweetness of some maple, and soon your guests will be licking their fingers.

1. Heat the oil in a pot over medium-high heat. Add the shallots and cook until soft, about 3 minutes.

2. Add the garlic and stir until fragrant, about 30 seconds.

3. Add the remaining ingredients and stir until well combined. Allow to cook until thickened, stirring occasionally, about 15 minutes.

4. Use immediately or store in an airtight container in the refrigerator for up to a week.

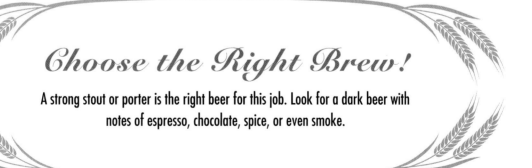

Choose the Right Brew!

A strong stout or porter is the right beer for this job. Look for a dark beer with notes of espresso, chocolate, spice, or even smoke.

Porter FIG JAM

1 CUP

FOR THE JAM:
2 cup dried figs, stems removed, chopped into thirds
2 tablespoons fresh lemon juice
½ cup white sugar
½ cup brown sugar
1⅓ cups porter, plus ¼ cup, if needed
¼ cup balsamic vinegar
1 teaspoon black pepper
1 teaspoon salt
¼ teaspoon smoked paprika

This jam walks the line between sweet and savory. It can be used inside pork loin, as a condiment on burgers and hot dogs, or as a fantastic addition to a breakfast biscuit.

1. In a pot over medium heat, add the figs, lemon juice, both kinds of sugar, 1⅓ cups beer, balsamic vinegar, pepper, salt, and smoked paprika.

2. Allow to simmer until thickened and the figs have softened and started to break down, about 25 minutes. Allow to cool slightly.

3. Add to a food processor; purée until smooth, about 3 minutes. Add additional beer and process again if mixture is too thick.

Choose the Right Brew!

Choose a dark and smoky beer: a porter or even a stout. Look for something with depth and just a touch of hops for the right notes to complement this jam.

Stout-BALSAMIC GLAZE

½ CUP

⅓ cup stout beer
⅔ cup balsamic vinegar
1 tablespoon honey

This glaze is beautiful on so many things. It has a tart acidity as well as a deep sweetness and a mild note of malt from the stout. Use it on everything from roasted vegetables, grilled chicken, and even pizza.

1. In a saucepan over medium-high heat, add the stout, balsamic vinegar, and honey.

2. Allow to boil, stirring occasionally, until it has reduced and thickened, about 10 minutes.

3. Store in an airtight container in the refrigerator. Heat slightly before use if the sauce is too thick.

Choose the Right Brew!

Look for a malty stout with notes of chocolate and espresso for this.

Chapter 4

BREADS and PASTAS

Belgian White Ale English Muffin Loaf Bread ... 78

Chocolate, Bacon, and Porter Muffins ... 79

Classic Beer Bread ... 80

Drunken Carbonara Couscous ... 81

Hefeweizen Brioche Pull-Apart Dinner Roll Loaf ... 82

Loaded Beer Corn Bread ... 84

Pale Ale Corn Tortillas ... 85

Pale Ale Pasta Cavatelli ... 86

Pumpkin IPA Scones [M] ... 89

Roasted Garlic and Cheddar Beer Cheese Muffins ... 90

Pasta with Arugula, Tomatoes, and a Lemon-Beer Cream Sauce ... 92

Smoky Beer Mac and Cheese ... 94

Wheat Beer Sesame Hamburger
Buns ... 96

Belgian White Ale
ENGLISH MUFFIN LOAF BREAD

1 LOAF

2¼ cups bread flour
1 tablespoon sugar
2 tablespoons dry milk powder
½ teaspoon salt
1 packet rapid-rise yeast (do not use regular dry active yeast)
2 tablespoons unsalted butter
½ cup milk
½ cup wheat beer
Egg wash (1 egg whisked with 1 tablespoon water)

Choose the Right Brew!

A white ale will give you the bready notes you want. Look for a wheat beer with notes of cloves, spice, or oranges.

This is just like those little breakfast muffins, but in a loaf form. This is an easy recipe—no knead, just one rise—and it yields a surprisingly beautiful loaf that will make you some amazing morning toast and killer sandwiches later in the day. Using beer in bread gives a little extra power to the rise, which leaves you with light and airy bread that has a soft and tender texture.

1. Add flour, sugar, dry milk powder, salt, and yeast to a stand mixer fitted with a dough hook.

2. Melt the butter in a microwave-safe dish. Add the milk and beer, microwave for 30 seconds, test with a cooking thermometer, and repeat until liquid has reached 120°F–125°F.

3. Add the liquid to the mixer and mix on medium speed until the dough starts to gather around the blade, about 6 minutes. Dough will be very soft, almost batter-like.

4. Spray a 1½-quart loaf pan with cooking spray. Scrape the dough into prepared pan. Cover tightly with plastic wrap and allow to rise in a warm room until the dough is near the top of the loaf pan, about 1 hour.

5. Preheat the oven to 375°F. Brush the dough with egg wash. Bake at 375°F for 23–27 minutes or until the bread is a dark golden brown.

Chocolate, Bacon, and
PORTER MUFFINS

8 MUFFINS

½ cup unsweetened cocoa powder
1 cup flour
¾ cup sugar
¼ teaspoon salt
1 teaspoon baking powder
¼ teaspoon smoked paprika
1 egg
¼ cup canola oil
¾ cup smoked porter
½ cup dark chocolate chips
3 strips of bacon, cooked and chopped

Beer for breakfast? Yes! Bacon, chocolate, and beer make this muffin a combination of all the world's best foods. You won't be able to keep your hands off these. With these easy and quick preparations, you'll end up making this for every meal.

1. Preheat oven to 400°F.

2. In a large bowl, combine the cocoa powder, flour, sugar, salt, baking powder, and smoked paprika. Whisk until well combined.

3. In a separate bowl, beat the egg and the oil. Make a well in the dry ingredients and add the egg, oil, beer, and chocolate chips. Stir until combined.

4. Spray muffin tins with butter-flavored cooking spray (or line with muffin papers). Add the batter to the muffin tins until about ⅔ full. Top with the chopped bacon, evenly distributed between the muffin tins.

5. Bake for 18–22 minutes or until the tops spring back when touched.

Choose the Right Brew!

A smoked porter is a great way to go, but they can be hard to find. Look far and wide and you'll be able to track one down. Don't worry—you'll be handsomely rewarded with the world's most amazing muffins. If you can't get your hands on one, look for a porter or a stout with notes of chocolate or espresso.

Classic BEER BREAD

1 LOAF

3 cups all-purpose flour
2 tablespoons sugar
1 tablespoon baking powder
¼ teaspoon salt
1½ cups wheat beer
4 tablespoons melted unsalted butter,
  plus 2 tablespoons, divided

Bread baking doesn't get any easier than this. It's really just a mix–and–dump batter that takes you five minutes to prepare before you throw it in the oven. The spoils of your Bread Baking Triumph will give you a killer grilled cheese sandwich, or unforgettable French toast. It's also the perfect vehicle for some butter and jam.

1. Preheat oven to 375°F.

2. Add flour, sugar, baking powder, and salt to a bowl; stir until combined.

3. Add beer and 4 tablespoons melted butter. Stir until just combined (some lumps are fine).

4. Lightly spray a large 1½-quart loaf pan with cooking spray. Add dough to prepared pan.

5. Top with remaining melted butter.

6. Bake at 375°F for 40–45 minutes or until golden brown.

Choose the Right Brew!

A wheat beer is a great way to go for this dish, but this classic recipe also lends itself well to various styles of beer. An IPA will give you a bolder beer taste, and brown ale will give you a malty, possibly even nutty flavor. Blonde ales and pilsner will work just fine as well.

Drunken CARBONARA COUSCOUS

4 SERVINGS

⅔ cup chicken broth
⅔ cup white ale
1 cup pearl couscous
1 cup diced pancetta or bacon, raw
1 tablespoon unsalted butter
1 cup chopped beefsteak or heirloom
  tomatoes
⅓ cup grated or shaved Parmesan
  cheese
1 teaspoon fresh cracked black pepper
4 large eggs
Salt and pepper

Carbonara is a classic Italian recipe that combines the goodness of bacon, Parmesan, and egg, all stirred up with some pasta. I've added some beer to the pearl couscous and topped it with a poached egg so your guests can break the yolk and watch Nature's Perfect Sauce run into the rest of the dish. Interactive food is just more fun.

1. In a pot over medium-high heat, add the chicken broth and beer and bring to a boil. Add the couscous, stir for about 2 minutes, cover, and turn off heat. Let sit until couscous has cooked through and all of the liquid has absorbed, about 10 minutes.

2. In a separate pan, cook the pancetta or bacon. Drain off about half the fat, leaving about 3 tablespoons still in the pan with the pork. Add the butter and cook until melted; remove from heat. Add the couscous and toss to coat. Add the tomatoes, Parmesan, and pepper; stir to combine.

3. One or two at a time, poach eggs in simmering water until whites have set but yolk is still runny.

4. Divide couscous between 4 bowls. Top each bowl with a poached egg. Salt and pepper to taste, if desired. Serve immediately.

Choose the Right Brew!

The bready and citrus notes of a white ale work well to counterbalance the richness of the pork and cheese in this recipe. Look for a white ale with notes of bread, citrus, and even basil.

Hefeweizen BRIOCHE PULL-APART DINNER ROLL LOAF

MAKES 2 LOAVES OR 16 ROLLS

4 cups bread flour
2 packets rapid-rise yeast
2 tablespoons sugar
⅓ cup heavy cream
½ cup hefeweizen (or other wheat beer)
2 large eggs, room temperature
2 tablespoons honey
1 teaspoon salt
1 cup unsalted butter, softened to room temperature, cut into cubes
Egg wash (1 egg whisked with 1 tablespoon water)

This is where hefeweizen proves its baking chops. A smooth wheat beer gives these unforgettable rolls a light and creamy texture with hints of honey. This recipe took about two years to develop, and now that it's finalized, these will be the rolls I place on my holiday table for the rest of my bread-making life. The rolls bake side by side in a loaf pan and come out of the oven looking like a bubble-top bread loaf that is just 8 beautiful rolls stuck together, waiting to be pulled off and enjoyed.

1. In the bowl of a stand mixer fitted with a dough hook, add the flour, yeast, and sugar. Stir to combine.

2. Add the cream and beer to a microwave-safe bowl. Microwave on high for 25 seconds, test temperature with a cooking thermometer, and repeat until liquid is between 120°F and 130°F.

3. Add the liquid to the flour and mix on medium speed until incorporated and slightly dry stringy lumps form.

4. Add the eggs one at a time, mixing well between each addition. Then add the honey and the salt.

5. About ¼ cup at a time, add the butter, mixing well between each addition. The dough will be very soft.

6. Mix on medium-high speed until the dough gathers around the dough hook, 6–8 minutes.

7. Remove from the mixer and place in a lightly oiled bowl. Cover tightly with plastic wrap and set in a warm room until the dough is doubled in size, 1½–2 hours.

8. Set dough on a lightly floured surface, cut into 2 equal pieces. Each of these pieces will be a separate loaf.

9. Cut each loaf into 8 equal pieces.

10. One at a time, flatten each dough piece into a 6" circle (resembling a small tortilla).

11. Form into a tight ball by grabbing the edges and pulling them into the center.

12. Place the dough balls, smooth side up, into two large 1½-quart loaf pans that have been sprayed with cooking spray. Place 8 dough balls into each pan in 2 parallel rows of 4 balls each.

13. Cover tightly with plastic wrap and allow to rise until almost doubled in size, about 1 hour.

14. Preheat oven to 375°F. Brush the tops of each loaf with egg wash. Bake at 375°F for 20–26 minutes or until a golden brown.

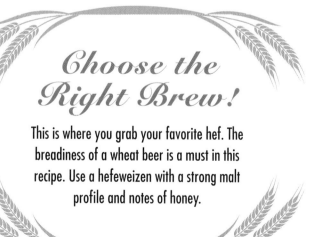

Choose the Right Brew!

This is where you grab your favorite hef. The breadiness of a wheat beer is a must in this recipe. Use a hefeweizen with a strong malt profile and notes of honey.

Loaded Beer CORN BREAD

MAKES 1 LOAF OR 12–13 MUFFINS

1 cup cake flour
¼ cup brown sugar
1 cup yellow cornmeal
1 tablespoon baking powder
½ teaspoon salt
1 ear of corn (1 cup of kernels; if using frozen corn, thaw prior to use)
1 jalapeño, stemmed, seeded, and chopped
2½ weight ounces sharp Cheddar, shredded (about ¾ cup)
⅔ cup wheat beer
⅓ cup buttermilk
¼ cup melted unsalted butter plus 2 tablespoons, divided
1 tablespoon vegetable oil
1 large egg
2 tablespoons melted unsalted butter
4 strips of thick sliced bacon, cooked and chopped

Corn bread can be a meal all in itself—especially when it's filled with bacon, cheese, and peppers. It's also a great accompaniment to a hearty chili or beef stew.

1. Preheat oven to 375°F.

2. In a large bowl, add the flour, brown sugar, yellow cornmeal, baking powder, and salt, stirring to combine.

3. Cut the kernels off the ear of corn. This should be about 1 cup of kernels.

4. Add the corn, jalapeño, and Cheddar to the dry ingredients.

5. In a separate bowl whisk together the beer, buttermilk, ¼ cup melted butter, oil, and egg.

6. Add the wet ingredients to the dry ingredients and stir until just combined.

7. Spray a large loaf pan, an 8" × 8" baking pan, or a muffin tin with cooking spray. Pour batter into prepared pan.

8. Pour remaining melted butter evenly over the pan. Sprinkle with chopped bacon.

9. Bake at 375°F for 23–26 minutes (12–15 for muffins) or until the top is just starting to turn golden brown and a toothpick inserted in the center comes out with just a few crumbs.

Choose the Right Brew!

An unfiltered wheat beer will give you a nice rounded flavor for this cornbread. If you choose a higher-hopped beer, you'll get a more exaggerated beer flavor, so proceed with caution.

Pale Ale CORN TORTILLAS

16–18 TORTILLAS

2 cups masa harina
½ teaspoon salt
1⅓ cups wheat beer or pale ale,
  room temperature

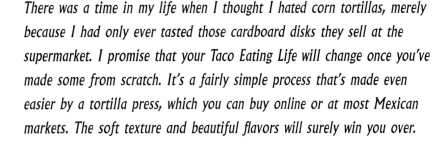

Choose the Right Brew!

I love a pale ale with a balanced malt-to-hop ratio and an earthy or piney flavor for these tortillas.

There was a time in my life when I thought I hated corn tortillas, merely because I had only ever tasted those cardboard disks they sell at the supermarket. I promise that your Taco Eating Life will change once you've made some from scratch. It's a fairly simple process that's made even easier by a tortilla press, which you can buy online or at most Mexican markets. The soft texture and beautiful flavors will surely win you over.

1. In a large bowl, add the masa harina and the salt and stir to combine. Add the beer and stir to combine. A good tortilla dough should have the consistency of Play-Doh. If the dough is too dry to hold together, add additional beer or water. If it is too wet, add more masa harina. Form into balls about the size of golf balls.

2. Place two small sheets of parchment paper inside the tortilla press to act as a barrier between the press and the masa dough.

3. Place one ball of dough on a sheet of parchment in the center of the tortilla press, top with the second sheet and press until tortilla is flat. In lieu of a tortilla press, you can roll out tortillas with a rolling pin into 6" disks on a flat surface that has been dusted with masa harina.

4. Heat an electric griddle to 350°F, or heat a skillet over medium-high heat. Cook the tortilla until just slightly browned on the bottom (about 30 seconds to 1 minute); flip and cook on the other side. Don't overcook. Use immediately or store in an airtight container in the fridge for up to 3 days.

Note: Masa harina is sold in most commercial grocery stores in the Mexican food aisle.

Pale Ale PASTA CAVATELLI

3 CUPS

2 cups all-purpose flour
1 cup semolina flour
½ teaspoon salt
1 cup warm pale ale or wheat beer

This homemade pasta recipe doesn't require any special equipment. No rollers, machines, or even a mixer. Even though it's labor intensive, you will earn the supreme satisfaction of being able to start sentences with, "This one time, when I was making pasta from scratch . . ." Even better, these can be made ahead and stored in an airtight for up to a month until ready for use.

1. Add both kinds of flour and salt to a flat surface and mix to combine.

2. Make a well in the middle and add the beer. Stir the liquid and the flour together until combined. Then knead until smooth, about 5 minutes.

3. Cut into 6 pieces, wrap individually in plastic wrap, and chill in the refrigerator for 1 hour.

4. Lightly dust a baking sheet with flour. Set aside.

5. One at a time, take the pieces of dough and form into long logs ¼"–½" in diameter. Cut off about ¼" slice (it should be about the size of a dime) and place it in front of you on a flat but slightly textured surface, like wood. If the surface is too smooth, the cavatelli won't form well.

6. Place the flat edge of a bench knife or the dull side of a butter knife on the far side of the dough circle. Pull the knife toward you, smearing the dough against the counter. The dough should curl up over the knife and look like a little canoe. Place cavatelli on the floured baking sheet until ready to cook. (If you won't be cooking it immediately, allow it to dry completely and then store it in an airtight container for up to a month until ready to use.)

7. Cook in lightly salted simmering water until al dente, about 6 minutes.

Choose the Right Brew!

A pale ale is a safe bet, but you can also grab a wheaty hefeweizen for some added bready notes. Just stick to the lighter end of the beer spectrum. Porters and stouts are better used elsewhere.

Pumpkin IPA SCONES [M]

12 SCONES

FOR SCONES:
3⅓ cups flour
½ cup white sugar, plus 1 tablespoon, divided
¼ cup brown sugar
½ teaspoon salt
1 teaspoon cinnamon
¼ teaspoon nutmeg
3 teaspoons baking powder
6 tablespoons unsalted butter, cut into cubes
½ cup pumpkin purée
½ cup IPA beer
1 egg, lightly beaten
2 tablespoons melted unsalted butter

FOR GLAZE:
1 cup powdered sugar
1 tablespoon IPA beer
1 tablespoon whole milk or cream

Scones often find themselves in the breakfast category, but these make a fine afternoon snack or a nice finish to a rich meal. With a hint of high-hop beer and a mellow but strong pumpkin flavor, these pastries make a great coffee companion any time of year.

1. Preheat oven to 400°F.

2. To make the scones, in a food processor combine flour, ½ cup white sugar, brown sugar, salt, cinnamon, nutmeg, and baking powder. Pulse a few times to combine. Add 6 tablespoons butter and process until the mixture is combined and resembles coarse meal.

3. Transfer mixture to a bowl. Using your hands or a wooden spoon, stir in the pumpkin purée, beer, and beaten egg.

4. Transfer to a well-floured surface and turn a few times until the dough comes together. Pat into a circle about 1" in thickness. Cut into 12 wedges.

5. Place on a baking sheet covered with parchment paper. Brush with melted butter and sprinkle with remaining tablespoon of sugar.

6. Bake at 400°F until golden brown, about 15 minutes. Remove from oven and cool to just above room temperature before glazing.

7. To make the glaze, in a small bowl whisk together the powdered sugar, 1 tablespoon beer, and whole milk or cream. Dip the top of each scone into the glaze and return to parchment until the glaze has set. Serve immediately.

Choose the Right Brew!

The starch and sugars tame a high-hop brew. Although a small amount of beer is called for in this recipe, the hop flavors come through with a bold beer. The best IPA for this is one with floral and citrus notes. You can also try your favorite pumpkin ale here.

Roasted Garlic
AND CHEDDAR
BEER CHEESE MUFFINS

MAKES 12 MUFFINS

1 head garlic
1 tablespoon olive oil
½ cup whole milk
½ cup pale ale
2 large eggs
3 tablespoons unsalted butter, melted
1 cup freshly grated sharp Cheddar
   (don't use preshredded)
2 cups all-purpose flour
2 teaspoons baking powder
1 tablespoon sugar
½ teaspoon salt
½ teaspoon chili powder

This single–serving size beer bread is loaded up with roasted garlic and Cheddar to give it warmth and depth that gives these muffins an unforgettable flavor. Great anytime of day, these savory muffins are great to serve with dinner or with a breakfast spread.

1. Preheat oven to 425°F.

2. Cut the pointed tip off the head of garlic, exposing the cloves. Place the garlic head on a small sheet of aluminum foil. Drizzle with olive oil and fold into a tight packet. Place garlic packet in a baking dish and roast at 425°F for 25–30 minutes, or until soft and the cloves have turned an amber color. Lower oven temperature to 350°F.

3. In a large bowl whisk together the milk, beer, and eggs. Add the butter and whisk. Squeeze the head of garlic until the cloves come out. They should be very soft and have an almost paste-like consistency. Add to the batter and whisk until cloves are broken up and well mixed. Add the cheese and stir.

4. Sprinkle the flour, baking powder, sugar, salt, and chili powder into the bowl; gently stir.

5. Spray muffin tins with cooking spray.

6. Pour batter into muffin tins until about ⅔ full.

7. Place in the oven. Lower temperature to 325°F and bake for 20–25 minutes or until the tops spring back when touched.

Choose the Right Brew!

This is a job for a pale ale. The higher the hop level, the higher the beer taste—the decision is yours. If you want a low, mild beer flavor, grab a lower-hopped pale ale, a wheat beer, or a clean, crisp pilsner. If you want a kick-you-in-the-face beer taste, grab the highest IBU IPA you can find.

PASTA WITH ARUGULA, TOMATOES, AND A *Lemon-Beer Cream Sauce*

4 SERVINGS

||||||||||||||||||||||||||||||||||||||||||||||||||||||||||

1 teaspoon unsalted butter

2 tablespoons minced shallot

1 cup pale ale beer

1 cups chicken or vegetable broth

1 teaspoon fresh oregano or basil, chopped

½ cup heavy cream

1 tablespoon lemon juice

1 teaspoon fine lemon zest

2 tablespoons grated Parmesan cheese

¼ teaspoon kosher or sea salt

½ teaspoon freshly ground black pepper

2 cups dry cavatelli, farfalle, or orecchiette pasta

1 beefsteak tomato, chopped (about 1½ cups)

1 cup baby arugula, chopped

I've been told that the secret to great pasta noodles is to finish the cooking process in the sauce with which you intend to serve them. It's a pretty brilliant tip: The starch of the noodles thickens the sauce a bit, while the sauce works its way into the noodles. This dish is a great example of that. After tasting it, I hope you continue to use this advice in preparing your pasta dishes.

1. In a large saucepan or skillet over medium-high heat, melt the butter. Add the shallots and cook until softened but not browned, about 3 minutes.

2. Add the beer and broth. Bring to a gentle boil, stirring occasionally, until reduced by half, 10–12 minutes.

3. Turn off heat, stir in oregano or basil and cream, and return to a gentle boil for an additional 6–8 minutes until reduced and slightly thickened.

4. Remove from heat; add the lemon juice, lemon zest, cheese, salt, and pepper; and stir to combine.

5. While sauce is cooking, cook the pasta in lightly salted boiling water until nearly cooked, about 3 minutes less than package directions state. Drain.

6. Add the pasta to the sauce and return to a gentle simmer. Cook until the pasta is al dente and sauce has thickened, about 3–5 minutes. Remove from heat, add tomatoes and arugula, and toss to combine.

Choose the Right Brew!

A beer on the paler end of the scale will serve you well with this. Look for a beer with a medium-hop profile and notes of citrus. A pale ale, a honey bock, or even a hoppy wheat beer would all work. Too high a hop profile might leave you with too much bitterness, but the sweetness of the tomatoes and the bite of arugula round out a medium-hopped beer.

Smoky Beer MAC AND CHEESE

SERVES 6–8

½ cup unsalted butter
3 tablespoons flour
3 cups whole milk
2 cups pale ale
2 teaspoons mustard powder
½ teaspoon chili powder
6 weight ounces (1½ cups shredded) sharp smoked Cheddar, shredded (do not use preshredded)
6 weight ounces (1½ cups shredded) sharp white Cheddar, shredded (do not use preshredded)
8 weight ounces (2 cups shredded) smoked Gouda, shredded (do not use preshredded)
4 cups large elbow macaroni
1 teaspoon kosher salt
Fresh black pepper
1 cup panko breadcrumbs
3 tablespoons melted unsalted butter

Everyone needs to have a fantastic mac and cheese recipe in their back pocket. This is an extra-creamy version with a hint of smokiness. Cooking the noodles in the sauce is the secret weapon when it comes to keeping that cheesiness alive all the way to the plate.

1. Preheat oven to 350°F.

2. In a large pot or Dutch oven, melt the butter over medium-high heat. Sprinkle with flour; whisk until a paste forms.

3. Add milk and beer; bring to a simmer.

4. Sprinkle with mustard powder and chili powder.

5. Slowly add the cheese, about ¼ cup at a time, whisking each addition until well combined before adding more. Reserve ½ cup of cheese (combination of all three cheeses) for the topping.

6. Add the noodles to the cheese sauce, allowing to cook until al dente but not cooked through, stirring occasionally, about 10 minutes. Stir in salt and pepper.

7. Lightly spray a 4-quart baking dish with cooking spray; pour the macaroni and the cheese sauce into the prepared dish in an even layer.

8. Top with remaining cheese.

9. Toss panko with melted butter until well coated. Sprinkle panko evenly on the top of the macaroni.

10. Bake at 350°F until panko has browned, about 25–30 minutes.

Choose the Right Brew!

If you can get your hands on a smoky pale ale, you've hit the jackpot. If you can't, look instead for a medium-hopped pale ale with floral notes to balance out some of that smoke.

Wheat Beer
SESAME HAMBURGER BUNS

8 BUNS

3½ cups all-purpose flour
2 tablespoons sugar
1 package rapid-rise yeast
4 tablespoons unsalted butter, softened
¾ cup wheat beer
1 large egg
1¼ teaspoons salt
Egg wash (1 egg whisked with 1
    tablespoon water)
2 teaspoons onion powder
1 teaspoon salt
1 tablespoon sesame seeds

Nothing says love like a burger on a homemade bun. Take your next cookout to another level by making your burger buns from scratch. Your guests will be so impressed.

1. In the bowl of a stand mixer fitted with a paddle attachment, add the flour, sugar, and rapid-rise yeast; stir to combine.

2. Add the butter to a microwave-safe bowl; heat until melted. Add the beer, microwave on high for 15 seconds, check temperature with a cooking thermometer, and repeat until the liquid reaches 120°F–125°F.

3. Add the beer and butter to the stand mixer and beat until all the flour has been moistened.

4. Add the egg and salt, beating until the dough gathers around the blade.

5. Transfer to a lightly oiled bowl, cover tightly with plastic wrap, and allow to rise at room temperature until doubled in size, 60–90 minutes.

6. Punch down dough and remove it from bowl. Gently knead dough on a lightly floured surface for about 30 seconds.

7. Cut the dough into 2 equal pieces. Cut each of those in half to make 4 total, and then again to make 8.

8. Flatten each piece into a 6" circle. Starting at one end, roll the circle into a tight log to resemble a small cigar. Starting at the small end, roll the log to resemble a very small cinnamon roll.

9. Place bun, swirl side up, on a baking sheet covered with parchment paper. Press down firmly with the palm of your hand to flatten. Repeat for all dough pieces.

10. Cover tightly with plastic wrap and allow to rise until doubled, about 30 minutes.

11. Heat oven to 375°F. Brush buns with egg wash; sprinkle with onion powder, salt, and sesame seeds. Bake at 375°F until golden brown, 10–12 minutes.

Choose the Right Brew!

I like a citrusy Belgian white beer for these homemade buns, but any wheat beer will do. The added yeast and breadiness will be a fabulous complement to your homemade burger holder.

Chapter 5

VEGGIE-LOVERS ENTRÉES

Irish Red Ale Butternut Squash Bisque
with Goat Cheese and Pomegranate ... 100

Porter Black Bean Soup with Avocado Cilantro Cream ... 103

Pale Ale Caprese Pizza ... 104

Roasted Mushroom and Brown Ale Soup ... 106

Mushroom Stout Sliders with Chipotle Cream ... 108

Saison Ricotta, Roasted Tomatoes, and
Porter–Caramelized Shallots Galette ... 109

Irish Red Ale
BUTTERNUT SQUASH BISQUE WITH GOAT CHEESE AND POMEGRANATE

4 SERVINGS

1 (3½–4 pound) butternut squash
6 tablespoons olive oil, divided
1 head garlic
2 shallots, sliced
2½ cups vegetable broth
1 cup red ale
1 teaspoon salt
1 teaspoon pepper
¼ teaspoon turmeric
Pinch cayenne
½ cup heavy cream
3 weight ounces goat cheese
½ cup pomegranate seeds

The creaminess of goat cheese and the beautiful pop of acid from the pomegranate balances out the bite of beer for a well-rounded soup that will warm your winter bones. This soup isn't shy with the beer flavor, but if you want to tone it down a bit, choose a lower-hop beer.

1. Preheat oven to 425°F.

2. Cut the squash down the middle lengthwise; scoop out and discard seeds. Place cut side up on a baking sheet and drizzle with 2 tablespoons olive oil.

3. Cut the pointed tip off the head of garlic, exposing the cloves. Place the garlic head on a small sheet of aluminum foil. Drizzle with olive oil and fold into a tight packet. Place garlic packet in a baking sheet with the squash.

4. Roast squash and garlic for 30 minutes. Remove the garlic and allow to cool. Continue to roast the squash until fork tender, another 20–30 minutes (total of about 1 hour). Remove from oven and allow to cool enough to handle. Gently scoop out the flesh (should be 4–4½ cups).

5. In a pot over medium heat, add the remaining 3 tablespoons olive oil and the shallots. Allow to cook, stirring occasionally, until the shallots have caramelized, 15–20 minutes (do not cook at too high heat or the shallots will burn). Add the broth and the beer and bring to a gentle simmer.

(continued)

6. Remove from heat. Add the roasted squash, salt, pepper, turmeric, cayenne, and cream, stirring until well combined.

7. Use an immersion blender to purée until smooth. (You can also work in batches to purée in a food processor or blender.) Return to heat. Allow to simmer for 10 minutes or until slightly thickened. Add broth to thin, if desired

8. Ladle into serving bowls; garnish with goat cheese and pomegranate.

Choose the Right Brew!

Irish reds are a fun bunch. Slightly sweet with toasty notes and a medium-hop profile, they really bring a rounded flavor to this soup. Look for a red (or even a brown ale or an amber) that has notes of caramel, nuts, and malt. Medium-hop profile is where you want to aim—too high and the flavors might be overwhelming.

Porter Black Bean Soup
WITH AVOCADO CILANTRO CREAM

SERVES 4–6

FOR THE SOUP:

1 pound dry black beans
2 tablespoons olive oil
1 white onion, chopped
1 red bell pepper, chopped
4 cloves garlic, minced
2 cups vegetable broth
24 fluid ounces porter
½ teaspoon smoked paprika
1 teaspoon black pepper
½ teaspoon salt

FOR THE CREAM SAUCE:

2 large ripe avocados
3 tablespoons veggie broth
2 teaspoons olive oil
¼ cup cilantro
¼ teaspoon salt
Pinch cayenne

A creamy, slightly smoky black bean soup with beer-flavored broth and creamy avocado cilantro cream is a perfect way to warm up on a cold day. It's vegan, gluten free, and full of flavor—the perfect pot for a group of diverse eaters.

1. Place black beans in a large bowl; cover with cold water and soak for 8 hours.

2. Heat 2 tablespoons olive oil in a large Dutch oven or stock pot and sauté the onions and red peppers until soft, about 3 minutes. Add the garlic and cook for about 30 seconds.

3. Add the broth, beer, and black beans and bring to a low simmer. Cover and cook until beans have softened, about 3 hours. Stir in the smoked paprika, pepper, and salt. Add additional broth or beer to thin, if desired.

4. In a food processor, add the avocados, broth, olive oil, cilantro, salt, and cayenne and process until smooth, about 3 minutes. Add additional broth to thin, if desired.

5. Ladle soup into bowls; top with avocado cream. Serve immediately.

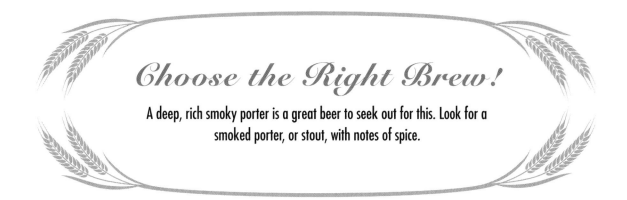

Choose the Right Brew!

A deep, rich smoky porter is a great beer to seek out for this. Look for a smoked porter, or stout, with notes of spice.

Pale Ale CAPRESE PIZZA

1 LARGE PIZZA

FOR THE BEER PIZZA DOUGH:
3 cups bread flour
¼ teaspoon salt
2 teaspoons sugar
1 cup wheat beer
1 packet dry active yeast
3 tablespoons whole milk
4 tablespoons olive oil, divided

FOR THE BEER PIZZA SAUCE:
2 tablespoons olive oil
1 shallot, minced
2 cloves garlic, minced
1½ cups IPA
1 (6-weight ounce) can tomato paste
1 teaspoon dried oregano
1 teaspoon dried basil
¼ teaspoon crushed red pepper

FOR THE STOUT BALSAMIC GLAZE:
⅓ cup stout beer
⅔ cup balsamic vinegar
1 tablespoon honey

FOR THE TOPPING:
3 weight ounces Parmesan, Pecorino-
   Romano, or Asiago cheese, grated
1 (8 weight ounce) ball of whole milk
   mozzarella, sliced into 6–8 slices
6 leaves fresh basil, chopped

Take a classic margherita pizza, drizzle it with a stout balsamic glaze, and voilà: a Caprese pizza. Beer leavens the dough and enhances the sauce and glaze. You can make this over several days, preparing the dough, sauce, and the glaze in advance. Then, simply pull everything together to impress your friends with the perfect Beer and Pizza Night offering.

1. To make the dough, in the bowl of a stand mixer fitted with a dough hook, add the bread flour, salt, and sugar; stir until well combined.

2. Add the beer to a microwave-safe bowl, microwave on high for 15 seconds, check temperature with a cooking thermometer, and repeat until the liquid reaches 110°F. Add the yeast and wait 5 minutes or until the yeast foams.

3. Add the beer and yeast to the mixer and stir on medium speed until incorporated.

4. Add the milk and 2 tablespoons oil. Mix on medium-high speed until the dough is soft and elastic and starts to gather around the hook, about 8 minutes. Place dough on a lightly floured surface; knead until smooth and no longer sticky, about 5 minutes.

5. Coat a large bowl with the remaining 2 tablespoons oil. Add the dough, cover, and refrigerate for 12 hours or until doubled in size.

6. Punch down the dough and reform into a tight ball. Cover and refrigerate for another 8–12 hours and up to 3 days.

7. To make the sauce, heat 2 tablespoons olive oil in a saucepan over medium-high heat. Add the shallots and cook until softened, about 3 minutes. Add the garlic and stir; cook for about 20 seconds before adding the beer, tomato paste, oregano, dried basil, and red pepper. Cook until thickened; then remove from heat. (Can be made up to 3 days ahead of time; refrigerate until ready to use.)

8. To make the glaze, in a saucepan over medium-high heat, add the stout, balsamic vinegar, and honey. Allow to boil, stirring occasionally, until it has reduced and thickened, about 10 minutes. (Glaze can be made up to 3 days ahead of time and stored in the fridge in an airtight container until ready to use. Heat slightly if too thick to drizzle.)

9. To assemble the pizza, place a pizza stone in the oven and preheat to 425°F for at least 30 minutes prior to baking pizza.

10. Roll out the pizza dough on a lightly floured surface to about the size of your pizza stone. Sprinkle a pizza peel with cornmeal. Transfer the dough to the pizza peel.

11. Spread pizza dough with pizza sauce. Sprinkle with Parmesan, Pecorino-Romano, or Asiago cheese. Place mozzarella slices evenly across the pizza.

12. Bake at 425°F for 8–10 minutes or until the crust turns golden brown. Remove from oven.

13. Drizzle with stout balsamic glaze; sprinkle with chopped basil.

Choose the Right Brew!

You'll need a beer trifecta for this. An unfiltered wheat beer makes a fantastic crust, a citrusy medium-hopped pale ale provides a fine match for the sauce, and a dark malty stout or porter adds just the right note to the glaze .

Roasted Mushroom
AND BROWN ALE SOUP

SERVES 4

3 weight ounces shiitake mushrooms, chopped (about 2 cups)
6 weight ounces portobello mushrooms, chopped (about 3 cups)
8 weight ounces white button mushrooms, chopped (about 3 cups)
2 tablespoons olive oil
½ teaspoon salt
½ teaspoon pepper
2 tablespoons unsalted butter
1 tablespoon vegetable oil
1 white onion, chopped
¾ cup brown ale
4 cups vegetable broth
¼ cup heavy cream
½ teaspoon salt
½ teaspoon black pepper
¼ teaspoon smoked paprika

Roasting mushrooms can bring out the incredible flavors of those delicious little fungi. Add the nutty goodness of a good brown ale and you've got yourself a big bowl of comfort. This soup has a very mild beer flavor. If you want to crank that up a notch, use 1¼ cups of brown ale and 3½ cups of broth instead of the listed amounts.

1. Preheat oven to 425°F. Place mushrooms on a baking sheet; toss with olive oil, salt, and pepper. Roast for 8 minutes. Toss and roast for an additional 8 minutes or until dark brown.

2. In a large pot over medium-low heat, add butter and vegetable oil. Add onions and cook until caramelized, stirring occasionally, 15–20 minutes.

3. Add the beer, scraping to deglaze the pan. Add the mushrooms and the broth; simmer for 10 minutes.

4. Remove from heat. Using an immersion blender, purée until smooth.

5. Slowly stir in the cream. Add the salt, pepper, and smoked paprika. Serve immediately.

Choose the Right Brew!

A nutty brown ale is the right beer for this dish. The malty, low-hop nuttiness is a great complement to these roasted mushroomy flavors.

Mushroom Stout Sliders
WITH CHIPOTLE CREAM

12 SLIDERS

3 tablespoons olive oil

1 large shallot, sliced

2 cloves garlic, minced

16 weight ounces crimini mushrooms, thinly sliced

2 tablespoons balsamic vinegar

½ cup stout beer, plus 1 tablespoon, divided

¼ teaspoon salt

½ teaspoon black pepper

1 cup sour cream

1 small chipotle pepper in adobo sauce

12 slider buns (or small dinner rolls, split)

Mushrooms are one of nature's best "meats." I spent three years as a vegetarian and discovered that the joys of mushrooms made processed meat replacements unnecessary in my kitchen. Even though I now partake in carnivorous meals, a great mushroom can still make me forget about steak.

1. In a skillet over medium-high heat, add the oil. Sautee the shallots until soft, about 3 minutes.

2. Add the garlic and mushrooms; sauté until the mushrooms have darkened, about 5 minutes.

3. Add the balsamic vinegar, ½ cup stout, salt, and pepper and simmer until the pan is mostly dry and the mushrooms are very soft. Remove from heat.

4. Add the sour cream, chipotle, and remaining 1 tablespoon stout to a food processor and process until smooth.

5. Warm the slider buns slightly. Fill buns with mushrooms; top with chipotle cream. Serve immediately.

Choose the Right Brew!

Look for a dark beer—porter or stout, for instance—that has earthy, malty notes to bring out the "meaty" quality in the mushrooms.

Saison Ricotta, ROASTED TOMATOES, AND PORTER–CARAMELIZED SHALLOTS GALETTE

SERVES 4–6

FOR THE CRUST:
2 cups all-purpose flour, divided
1 teaspoon salt
1 teaspoon sugar
¾ cup unsalted butter
⅓ cup ice-cold wheat beer
2 tablespoons melted unsalted butter

FOR THE RICOTTA:
1 quart whole milk (pasteurized is fine; ultrapasteurized will not work)
½ cup heavy cream
½ teaspoon salt
½ cup wheat beer
3 tablespoons lemon juice

FOR THE FILLING:
½ cup shallots sliced into ⅛" rings (2–3 large shallots)
2 tablespoons unsalted butter
1 tablespoon oil
⅓ cup porter beer
1 cup grape tomatoes
½ cup Parmesan cheese, fresh grated
1 cup arugula

This casual but elegant meal has the unpretentiousness of a pizza but the sophistication of a tart—and it's easier to create. The homemade ricotta comes together in about 15 minutes and can be made in advance. Similarly, the no–fuss dough for the crust can be made ahead of time, and it doesn't even need to rise. The final result? An impressive way to handle a dinner crowd.

1. To make the crust, in a food processor add 1⅓ cups flour, salt, sugar, and butter; process until well combined.

2. Add the remaining flour and process again until combined.

3. Transfer mixture from food processor to a bowl. Mix in the beer until just combined. Dough will be soft.

4. Form dough into a wide flat disk, wrap in plastic wrap, and chill for at least 2 hours. Can be made 3 days ahead of time.

5. To make the ricotta, in a pot over medium-high heat add the milk, cream, salt, and ½ cup beer.

6. Clip a cooking thermometer onto the side of the pan. Bring the liquid to 180°F, stirring occasionally to prevent the bottom from scorching.

7. Remove from heat, add the lemon juice, and stir gently once or twice. It should curdle immediately.

8. Allow to sit undisturbed for about 5 minutes.

9. Line a large strainer with 1 or 2 layers of cheesecloth, and place the strainer in the sink over a large bowl.

(continued)

10. Pour the ricotta into the strainer and allow to drain for 15–60 minutes. The longer the drain time, the firmer the ricotta will be.

11. Refrigerate until ready to use (can be made up to 5 days in advance).

12. To make the filling, in a skillet over medium heat, add the shallots, 2 tablespoons butter, and 1 tablespoon oil.

13. Cook for 5 minutes, or until the shallots start to soften; add beer. Cook, stirring occasionally, until caramelized, 15–18 minutes.

14. Preheat oven to 375°F.

15. On a lightly floured surface, add the dough; sprinkle with additional flour. Roll into a rustic 16" circle; transfer dough to a sheet of parchment paper.

16. Spread with ricotta cheese, leaving a 3–4" empty border. Top ricotta with caramelized shallots, then with grape tomatoes and Parmesan.

17. Fold the empty dough up over the filling, leaving an opening in the middle of the galette.

18. Move parchment and galette to a baking sheet. Brush with melted butter.

19. Bake at 375°F for 35–40 minutes or until golden brown. Top with arugula prior to serving.

Choose the Right Brew!

For the crust and the ricotta, stick to a citrusy wheat beer; the bready and yeast qualities come through beautifully. For the caramelized onions, look for a porter with notes of smoke or pepper.

Chapter 6

BEEF and PORK

Beer-Braised Pulled-Pork Tacos with Beer Corn Tortillas ... 115

Beer-Braised Short Rib Sliders with Quick Pickled Slaw ... 117

Steak with Stout Portobello Mushroom Sauce ... 118

Beer-Marinated Flank Steak with IPA Chimichurri [M] ... 119

Chorizo Stout Sloppy Joes ... 121

IPA-Marinated Pork Chops with Stout Cherry Sauce ... 122

Pig Newton Beer Burger ... 123

Porter-Braised Pulled-Pork Sandwiches with IPA Jalapeño Slaw [M] ... 126

Porter Osso Buco ... 129

Slow-Roasted Maple Stout Baby Back Beef Ribs ... 130

Stout and Stilton Beef Empanadas ... 133

Porter, Goat Cheese, and Portobello
Mushroom–Stuffed Pork Loin ... 135

Beer-Braised PULLED-PORK TACOS WITH BEER CORN TORTILLAS

14–16 TACOS

FOR THE PORK:
3-pound pork shoulder
6 cloves garlic, peeled
2 tablespoons kosher or sea salt
2 tablespoons brown sugar
1 teaspoon black pepper
1 teaspoon smoked paprika
2 teaspoons chili powder
½ teaspoon cayenne pepper
2 teaspoons onion powder
2 tablespoons olive oil
24 fluid ounces stout beer
2 cups beef broth

FOR THE BEER TORTILLAS
(makes 14–16 tortillas):
2 cups masa harina
½ teaspoon salt
1⅓ cups room temperature wheat beer
   or pale ale

FOR THE GARNISH:
½ cup cilantro, chopped
1 white onion, chopped

Everyone loves taco night. Add in the delicious meat–tenderizing properties of a good malty stout and Taco Tuesdays will never be the same. Oh, and you'll be the rock star who makes tortillas from scratch . . . with beer.

1. Preheat oven 300°F.

2. To prepare the pork, using a paring knife, create 6 2"-deep holes evenly spaced through the meat. Push a peeled clove of garlic into each hole until garlic is no longer visible.

3. Sprinkle the pork evenly with salt.

4. In a small bowl mix together the brown sugar, pepper, paprika, chili powder, cayenne, and onion powder. Rub the spices all over the surface of the pork.

5. In a large oven-safe pot or Dutch oven (with an oven-safe lid), heat the oil until hot but not smoking. Sear the meat on all sides, about 3 minutes per side.

6. Add the beer and broth and bring to a simmer.

7. Cover and place in the oven. Turn the meat over every 30–45 minutes. If the pot begins to dry out, add extra broth or hot water. Cook until meat is falling apart, 3–4 hours.

8. Remove from oven. Shred meat in pot, using two forks. Leave meat in the pan juices for 10 minutes while you prepare the tortillas. Remove meat from pan juices, draining off most of the liquid prior to serving.

(continued)

9. In a large bowl, add the masa harina and the salt and stir to combine. Add the beer and stir to combine. A good tortilla dough should have the consistency of Play-Doh. If the dough is too dry to hold together, add additional beer or water. If it is too wet, add more masa harina. Form into balls about the size of golf balls.

10. Place two small sheets of parchment paper inside the tortilla press to act as a barrier between the press and the masa dough.

11. Place one ball of dough on a sheet of parchment in the center of the tortilla press, top with the second sheet, and press until tortilla is flat. In lieu of a tortilla press, you can roll out tortillas with a rolling pin into 6" disks on a flat surface that has been dusted with masa harina.

12. Heat an electric griddle to 350°F, or heat a skillet over medium-high heat. Cook the tortilla until just slightly browned on the bottom (about 30 seconds to 1 minute); flip and cook on the other side. Don't overcook.

13. Fill the tortillas with pork and garnish with cilantro and onions.

Choose the Right Brew!

This is great way to use that stout you've had your eye on. Look for a dark beer with notes of spice, or check out a smoked stout or porter, which are starting to turn up in beer stores. Brewers are brilliant, aren't they?

Beer-Braised SHORT RIB SLIDERS WITH QUICK PICKLED SLAW

MAKES 12 SLIDERS

2 pounds bone-in short ribs
Salt and pepper
3 tablespoons olive oil
2 cups beef broth
12 fluid ounces stout beer
1 white onion, sliced
¼ cup Thai sweet chili sauce
¾ cup apple cider vinegar
¼ cup IPA beer
1 teaspoon salt
1 tablespoon sugar
6 whole allspice berries
1 teaspoon whole cloves
1 teaspoon whole black peppercorns
1 red onion, thinly sliced
1 cup cucumbers, peeled and sliced into
   matchstick-sized pieces
12 Hawaiian-style dinner rolls, split

A long cooking process with the meat–tenderizing property of beer gives these short ribs a beautiful texture. The acid of the pickled slaw and the sweetness of a soft Hawaiian roll make these the perfect party sandwich. Football season will never be the same.

1. Generously sprinkle short ribs with salt and pepper on all sides.

2. In a large pot or Dutch oven, heat the olive oil until hot but not smoking. Sear short ribs until browned on all sides, about 2 minutes per side.

3. Pour broth and stout over short ribs. Add the onion and sweet chili sauce and stir to combine. Cover and reduce heat to maintain a low simmer. Cook, stirring occasionally, until falling off the bone, about 2½ hours. Remove the bones.

4. While the short ribs are cooking, make the pickled slaw. In small saucepan over medium-high heat, combine apple cider vinegar, beer, salt, sugar, allspice, cloves, and peppercorns. Cook until sugar dissolves, then remove from heat. Cool to room temperature.

5. Strain the liquid to remove the cloves, peppercorns, and allspice. Pour strained liquid over the onions and cucumbers and refrigerate mixture for 30 minutes.

6. Fill the Hawaiian rolls with short ribs, topped with slaw.

Choose the Right Brew!

These short ribs need a strong stout. Look for an imperial stout with
notes of coffee and spice.

STEAK WITH STOUT PORTOBELLO
Mushroom Sauce

SERVES 4

4 (5 weight ounce) steaks (1½" thick)
5 tablespoons unsalted butter
1 tablespoon olive oil
2 large portobello mushrooms, sliced
½ yellow onion, sliced
½ cup chicken broth
¾ cup stout beer
1 tablespoon Worcestershire sauce
Salt and pepper for seasoning

Choose the Right Brew!

This is no job for a pale ale. Look for a dark stout or porter with notes of coffee, nuts, or chocolate to help you get the rich flavors this steak needs.

Steak and mushrooms get an extra dose of meatiness with a rich stout. Finishing the steak in the oven ensures that you get the doneness you want without burning the surface of your delicious steak.

1. Preheat oven to 350°F.

2. Remove the steaks from the refrigerator and allow them to come to room temperature, about 15 minutes.

3. In a pan over medium-high heat, add 3 tablespoons butter and olive oil and cook until butter has melted.

4. Add the mushrooms and onions, cooking until the mushrooms have darkened and the onions have softened, about 5 minutes.

5. Add the chicken broth, stout, and Worcestershire sauce and simmer until thickened, about 10 minutes.

6. In a separate pan, melt 2 tablespoons butter. Season the steaks liberally on each side with salt and pepper.

7. Once the butter is melted and hot (but not browned), add the steaks, two at a time. Cook until browned on each side, flipping only once, about 3 minutes per side.

8. Transfer to a baking dish or baking sheet. Place in the oven and cook for 6 minutes for medium rare, or until the internal temperature reaches 130°F.

9. Allow to rest for 5 minutes prior to serving. Serve the steaks topped with mushrooms.

Beer-Marinated
FLANK STEAK WITH IPA CHIMICHURRI [M]

SERVES 4

FOR THE MARINADE:
1 cup IPA beer
⅓ cup lime juice (about 2 large limes)
2 tablespoons olive oil
2 cloves garlic, chopped
1 teaspoon salt
1 teaspoon pepper
1 teaspoon cumin
2 pounds flank steak

FOR THE TOMATILLO CHIMICHURRI:
½ cup (packed) fresh Italian parsley
¼ cup olive oil
¼ cup IPA beer
⅔ cup (packed) fresh cilantro
1 large clove garlic, peeled
¼ cup chopped red bell pepper
1 cup tomatillos, husked and chopped
   (about 4–6)
½ teaspoon dried crushed red pepper
½ teaspoon salt
¼ teaspoon cumin
1 tablespoon lime juice

This dish will remind you of the powerful meat-tenderizing properties of beer. Even a traditionally tougher cut, such as a flank steak, will get a new life after hanging out in some beer for a while.

1. In a large bowl, stir together IPA, lime juice, olive oil, garlic, salt, pepper, and cumin. Add flank steak and allow to marinate at room temperature for 45–60 minutes (or refrigerate and marinate overnight).

2. In a food processor add the chimichurri ingredients; process until smooth.

3. Remove steak from marinade; drain well.

4. Preheat a grill, grill pan, or cast-iron skillet until very hot; brush with vegetable oil. Add the steak and cook on each side until medium rare, about 3–4 minutes per side.

5. Slice and serve topped with chimichurri sauce.

Choose the Right Brew!

Grab an IPA for this steak. Look for a high-hop beer with notes of citrus or spice. Alcohol intensifies heat, so the higher the ABV, the hotter the sauce will taste.

Chorizo Stout SLOPPY JOES

8 SANDWICHES

2 tablespoons olive oil
1 red bell pepper diced
½ cup white onion, diced
4 cloves garlic, minced
1 pound ground pork
12 weight ounces chorizo
1 cup stout beer
½ cup tomato paste
¼ teaspoon cumin
½ teaspoon black pepper
8 kaiser rolls
6 weight ounces cheese (Cheddar, Swiss, or pepper jack), sliced

Whether you're entertaining the school lunch lady or just fixing your typical weeknight dinner, Sloppy Joes make a fun and easy meal that you can throw together in a hurry. This is a great way to get some beer cookin' in when you don't have a lot of time.

1. In a skillet over medium-high heat, add the olive oil. Add the red bell pepper and white onions and cook until softened, about 5 minutes. Add the garlic and stir, cooking for about 30 seconds.

2. Add the ground pork and chorizo; cook until browned and mostly cooked through. Drain off most of the grease that has accumulated.

3. Add the stout, tomato paste, cumin, and black pepper and simmer until pork is cooked thoroughly, about 10 minutes.

4. Toast the buns in a warm skillet or toaster oven.

5. Scoop meat into kaiser rolls. Cover with cheese slices and tops of buns. Serve immediately.

Choose the Right Brew!

A dark beer with chili peppers is how you want to treat this dish. Brewers aren't shy about adding jalapeños, habaneros, chipotles, and even ghost chilies to their beers these days, and I couldn't be happier about it. Look for a chipotle stout or jalapeño porter or any dark beer with spicy notes.

IPA-MARINATED PORK CHOPS WITH
Stout Cherry Sauce

SERVES 4

1 cup IPA beer
1 cup buttermilk
1 teaspoon onion powder
1 teaspoon salt, divided
4 (4–6 weight ounce) boneless pork loin chops
1 cup panko breadcrumbs
1 cup flour
½ teaspoon pepper
Pinch cayenne
3 tablespoons unsalted butter
1 large shallot, sliced (about ½ cup)
2 cups pitted dark, sweet cherries (like Bing)
⅓ cup stout beer
½ teaspoon black pepper
3 tablespoons olive oil

Choose the Right Brew!

For the marinade look for a high-hop beer, like an IPA, with notes of citrus. For the cherry sauce, choose a malty stout with notes of fruit and cherries.

I finally figured out the secret to breaded pork chops: Ignore them. Bread them, set them out at room temperature, and forget them for about 20 minutes. This does two things. First, it gets each center closer to room temperature, which makes it easier to cook evenly and prevents a burnt crust and raw middle. Second, it helps the bread coating to adhere instead of slide off. Now you know the secret to perfect pork chops—temporary neglect.

1. In a large bowl combine the IPA, buttermilk, onion powder, and ½ teaspoon salt. Add the pork chops, cover, and refrigerate for 6–8 hours.

2. In a large bowl add the panko, flour, remaining ½ teaspoon salt, pepper, and pinch of cayenne. One at a time drain the pork chops and add to the bowl, tossing and pressing panko mixture into the pork until well coated.

3. Place on a sheet of wax paper or parchment paper. Allow to sit at room temperature for 20 minutes.

4. To make the cherry sauce, in a saucepan, melt the butter over medium heat. Add the shallots and cook until softened, about 5 minutes. Add the cherries, stout, and black pepper. Cook, stirring occasionally, until the cherries have broken down and the sauce has thickened, about 15 minutes.

5. To cook the pork chops, in a large skillet heat the olive oil. Fry the pork chops over medium-high heat until golden brown on each side and the internal temp is 145°F. Serve the pork chops topped with cherry sauce.

PIG NEWTON
Beer Burger

SERVES 8

FOR THE JAM:
2 cup figs (dried or fresh), stems removed, chopped
2 tablespoons fresh lemon juice
½ cup white sugar
½ cup brown sugar
1⅓ cups stout beer, plus ¼ cup, if needed
¼ cup balsamic vinegar
1 teaspoon black pepper
1 teaspoon salt
¼ teaspoon smoked paprika

FOR THE BURGERS:
3 pounds 90/10 ground beef
2 teaspoons salt
3 teaspoons black pepper
3 tablespoons stout beer
3 tablespoons Worcestershire sauce

FOR THE BUNS AND GARNISHES:
1 batch Wheat Beer Sesame Hamburger Buns (Chapter 4)
3 tablespoons melted unsalted butter
16 strips thick-cut bacon, cooked
4 weight ounces bleu cheese crumbles
1½ cups arugula

The addition of a homemade fig jam makes these bacon burgers fancy enough for a dinner party. Just like those pricy sirloin burgers at a steak house, these are fit for your upscale plates. Better yet, most of the components can be made in advance. Just don't forget to break out that $30 bottle of bourbon barrel–aged stout to serve alongside.

1. Start by making the jam. In a pot over medium heat, add the figs, lemon juice, both kinds of sugar, 1⅓ cups stout, balsamic vinegar, pepper, salt, and smoked paprika.

2. Simmer until thickened and the figs have softened and started to break down, about 25 minutes. Allow to cool slightly.

3. Add to a food processor; purée until smooth. If mixture is too thick, add additional stout and process.

4. Make the burger patties. In a medium bowl add the ground beef, salt, pepper, stout, and Worcestershire sauce and mix together until just combined. Avoid overworking the meat, which will make it tough. Form into 8 equal-sized patties, about ½"–¾" thick (can be made 12 hours in advance; refrigerate until ready to use).

(continued)

5. Grill or pan fry until medium-rare.

6. Split buns in half, brush with melted butter, and lightly toast on a grill or under a broiler until golden brown.

7. Spread each top bun with fig jam, and assemble each burgers with 2 slices of bacon, bleu cheese crumbles, and several leaves of arugula.

Choose the Right Brew!

This is a great recipe for a bourbon barrel–aged stout. Those amazing flavors of malt and bourbon pair nicely with figs and beef. If you can't find one, look for a stout with notes of smoke, espresso, or spice.

Porter-Braised
PULLED-PORK SANDWICHES WITH IPA JALAPEÑO SLAW [M]

SERVES 12

FOR THE PORK:
3-pound pork shoulder
6 cloves garlic, peeled
2 tablespoons kosher or sea salt
2 tablespoons brown sugar
1 teaspoon black pepper
1 teaspoon smoked paprika
2 teaspoons chili powder
2 teaspoons onion powder
2 tablespoons olive oil
24 fluid ounces stout beer
1 cup beef broth

Who doesn't love a good pulled–pork sandwich? Since beer acts as a meat tenderizer, using it for braising will up your pulled–pork game. Top this amazing sandwich with a spicy and tangy jalapeño slaw and you will have your guests eating out of your hand. Literally.

1. Preheat oven to 300°F.

2. Using a paring knife, create 6 2"-deep holes fairly evenly spaced through the meat. Push a peeled clove of garlic into each hole until garlic is no longer visible.

3. Sprinkle the pork evenly with salt.

4. In a small bowl mix together the brown sugar, pepper, paprika, chili powder, and onion powder. Rub the spices all over the surface of the pork.

5. In a large oven-safe pot or Dutch oven (with an oven-safe lid), heat the oil until hot but not smoking. Sear the meat on all sides, about 3 minutes per side.

6. Add the beer and broth; bring to a simmer.

7. Cover and place in the oven. Turn the meat over every 30–45 minutes. If the pot begins to dry out, add extra broth or hot water. Allow to cook until meat is falling apart, 3–4 hours.

(continued)

FOR THE IPA JALAPEÑO SLAW:

1 large jalapeño, stem and seeds
    removed, chopped (about ⅓ cup)
2 cups purple cabbage, thinly sliced
2 cups green cabbage, thinly sliced
¼ cup cilantro, chopped
½ cup sour cream
½ cup IPA
1 tablespoon lemon juice
1 tablespoon sugar
¼ teaspoon chili powder
¼ teaspoon salt
12 round kaiser roll sandwich buns

8. Remove from oven. Shred meat in pot, using two forks. Leave in the pan juices for 10 minutes while you prepare the jalapeño slaw.

9. To make the slaw, combine all ingredients in a medium-sized bowl; toss to coat.

10. Remove meat from pan juices, draining off most of the liquid prior to serving. Fill each sandwich bun with pork topped with slaw.

Choose the Right Brew!

This is a recipe that lends itself to many beer styles. I tend to lean toward a stout with notes of coffee or spice. Several breweries are making spicy stouts and porters with chipotle peppers; those are excellent choices for this recipe.

Porter OSSO BUCO

SERVES 4

FOR THE OSSO BUCO:

4 slices thick-cut bacon
1 teaspoon salt
1 teaspoon black pepper
¼ cup flour
2½ pounds beef shanks (4 or 5)
2 tablespoons olive oil
1½ cups carrots, peeled and sliced into
   ¼" coins (about 2 large)
2 ribs celery, chopped
1 cup white onions, chopped
1 cup porter
2 tablespoons tomato paste
3 cups beef broth

FOR THE GREMOLATA:

¼ cup fresh flat-leaf parsley, chopped
½ teaspoon lemon zest
½ teaspoon orange zest
1 large clove garlic, grated with a
   zester or microplane

Choose the Right Brew!

Rich dark porters and stouts with notes of espresso are great beers for this rich and meaty dish.

Osso buco means "bone with a hole" in Italian, referring to the glorious flavorful marrow in the center of the shanks. Although the traditional osso buco is made with veal, beef shanks will do just fine, especially after the meat–tenderizing property of beer has its way with this dish. Osso buco is traditionally served over rice, mashed potatoes, or polenta.

1. In a large pot or Dutch oven, cook the bacon over medium heat until most of the fat has rendered and the bacon starts to crisp. Turn off heat, remove bacon, and set aside; reserve bacon fat.

2. Add salt, pepper, and flour to a bowl; stir to combine. Pat the shanks dry and one at a time dredge in the flour until well coated.

3. Return the Dutch oven to medium-high heat until bacon fat is hot but not smoking. Sear the shanks in bacon fat until browned on both sides. Remove shanks from pot. Add olive oil to pot along with carrots, celery, and onion. Cook until softened, about 8 minutes.

4. Add the beer, scraping to deglaze the bottom. Stir in the tomato paste.

5. Return shanks and bacon to the pot. Pour in broth until shanks are ¾ covered, then reduce heat to maintain a low simmer.

6. While shanks are cooking, turn over every 20 minutes. Add additional broth to maintain a liquid level about ¾ of the way up the side of the shanks. Allow liquid to simmer but not boil for 3–3½ hours or until meat is tender and falling off the bone.

7. Add all gremolata ingredients in a small bowl, and toss to combine.

8. Serve shanks with pan sauce over polenta, rice, or mashed potatoes; top with gremolata.

Slow-Roasted MAPLE STOUT BABY BACK BEEF RIBS

SERVES 4

1 tablespoon olive oil
1 shallot, minced
4 cloves garlic, minced
½ cup low-sodium soy sauce
⅔ cup ketchup
2 tablespoons Worcestershire sauce
1 teaspoon red chili sauce
    (such as Sriracha)
2 teaspoons smoked paprika
1 cup stout beer
⅓ cup maple syrup
1 teaspoon onion powder
5 pounds baby back beef ribs
    (pork ribs will also work)
Salt

Good American barbecue is a thing of beauty. Slow-cooked, caramelized sugars, falling-off-the-bone tender meat in all of its messy, don't-wear-your-good-shirt splendor can only be accomplished with long, slow, and low cooking. If you don't own a giant barbecue contraption, you'll have to rely on your own oven to accomplish those slow-cooked flavors.

1. Preheat oven to 250°F.

2. Heat the oil in a pot over medium-high heat. Add the shallots and cook until soft, about 3 minutes. Add the garlic and stir until fragrant, about 30 seconds.

3. Add the soy sauce, ketchup, Worcestershire sauce, chili sauce, smoked paprika, stout, maple syrup, and onion powder and stir until well combined. Cook until thickened, stirring occasionally, about 15 minutes. Remove from heat.

4. Place the ribs on a baking sheet. Sprinkle on all sides with salt.

5. Brush liberally on all sides with barbecue sauce. Place in the oven and roast until falling off the bone, 3½–4 hours, turning and basting with barbecue sauce every 30–45 minutes.

Choose the Right Brew!

A good stout is the right man for this job. Choose something with notes of coffee, espresso, and even spice, if you can find it. A smoked porter or a chocolate stout will do a fabulous job as well.

Stout and Stilton
BEEF EMPANADAS

12 EMPANADAS

FOR THE DOUGH:
2¼ cups all-purpose flour
1 teaspoon salt
½ cup unsalted butter, cut into cubes
2 eggs, divided
⅓ cup pale ale

FOR THE FILLING:
2 tablespoons oil
1 large shallot, thinly sliced
2 cloves garlic, minced
2 cups cremini mushrooms, chopped
2 cups premium ground beef (85/15 lean-to-fat content)
½ cup stout beer, plus 2 tablespoons, divided
6 weight ounces blue Stilton cheese
½ teaspoon fresh cracked black pepper
½ teaspoon cumin

Nearly every country has their version of this savory handheld pie, which makes a comforting afternoon meal or a fantastic party appetizer. Just remember, however you serve it: Making the dough from scratch is a must since the flaky, buttery pastry is truly the star.

1. To make the dough, in a large bowl add the flour and salt; stir to combine. Add the butter and blend in with your fingers or a pastry blender until all of the butter has been incorporated.

2. In a small bowl add one of the eggs and the beer; beat with a fork until well blended.

3. Add egg mixture to the flour and stir until combined.

4. Add dough to a lightly floured surface. Cut into 12 equal-sized pieces, roll into balls, and place on a plate. Cover plate tightly with plastic wrap, and chill for at least one hour, and up to 24 hours.

5. To prepare the filling, heat the oil in a pan over medium-high heat. Add the shallots and cook until slightly caramelized, stirring occasionally, about 6 minutes. Add the garlic and mushrooms and cook until mushrooms have darkened, about 5 minutes.

6. Add the beef and ½ cup stout; cook until beef is cooked through. Drain off most of the liquid, leaving 1–2 tablespoons still in the pan.

(continued)

7. Add the remaining 2 tablespoons beer, cheese, pepper, and cumin. Stir over medium heat until cheese has mostly melted and combined.

8. Preheat oven to 375°F.

9. One at a time, roll out each dough ball into a 6" circle on a lightly floured surface.

10. Place about ¼ cup filling into the center of the circle, fold over, and press edges together well with your fingers. Seal edge with the tines of a fork. Place on a baking sheet that has been covered with parchment paper, or sprayed with cooking spray.

11. In a small bowl, beat the remaining egg. Brush each empanada with the egg.

12. Bake at 375°F for 25 minutes or until golden brown. Serve warm.

Choose the Right Brew!

You need two beers for this handheld treat. For the crust, look for a pale ale with a high ABV. The alcohol cooks off, making the pastry extra flaky. For the filling, look for a stout with coffee notes.

Porter, Goat Cheese, and PORTOBELLO MUSHROOM–STUFFED PORK LOIN

SERVES 4

1½-pound pork loin
1 cup porter, plus ½ cup, divided
2 slices thick-cut bacon, chopped
2 large portobello mushrooms, chopped (about 2½ cups)
½ teaspoon salt
½ teaspoon black pepper
¼ teaspoon smoked paprika
½ cup breadcrumbs
2 weight ounces goat cheese

Choose the Right Brew!

I love a smoked porter for this. If that is hard to come by, look for a stout or porter that has notes of espresso, spice, or nuts.

Marinating the pork loin in beer adds a touch of beer flavor, but most important, it tenderizes the meat. Porter also adds a beefy note to the pork as well as the mushrooms, creating a depth to the Other White Meat. Creamy goat cheese adds a nice tang to round out the flavors.

1. Place pork loin in a gallon-sized zip-top bag, and pour 1 cup of porter into the bag. Seal the bag, removing as much air as possible. Place in the refrigerator, marinate 2–4 hours.

2. In a pan over medium-high heat, cook the bacon until most of the fat has been rendered and the bacon is about halfway cooked. Add the mushrooms and cook until darkened and softened, about 8 minutes.

3. Add ½ cup porter, salt, pepper, and smoked paprika and cook until most of the beer has been absorbed. Turn off heat; stir in breadcrumbs and goat cheese.

4. Remove pork from marinade. Cut the loin down the center lengthwise about ¾ of the way through, making sure not to cut all the way through. Open the pork like a book. Cover with plastic wrap and pound to an even ½" thickness with a meat mallet or rolling pin.

5. Spread mushroom filling evenly across the pork loin. Starting at the long side, roll the pork loin tightly; secure with kitchen twine. Sprinkle all sides with additional salt and pepper.

6. Place on a baking sheet that has been covered with aluminum foil. Bake at 375°F for 40–50 minutes or until the internal temperature has reached 140°F. Let rest for 5 minutes before slicing and serving.

Chapter 7
THINGS with WINGS

Beer-Braised Chipotle Chicken with Red Peppers over
Drunken Cilantro Lime Rice...138

Beer Marinara Turkey Meatball Sandwiches...140

Brown Ale–Brined Roast Turkey...142

Brown Sugar and Brown Ale Niçoise Chicken Thighs...144

Honey Mustard Pale Ale Chicken...146

Beer-Brined Salt-Roasted Chicken...147

Paprika Chicken with Roasted Red Pepper Cream Sauce [M]...148

Porter-Glazed Asian Chicken Meatballs...150

Stout and Cheddar Chicken Potpie...152

White Bean and Beer Chicken Chili...153

Stout and Pomegranate–Glazed
Chicken Wings...154

Beer-Braised CHIPOTLE CHICKEN WITH RED PEPPERS OVER DRUNKEN CILANTRO LIME RICE

SERVES 4

|||||||||||||||||||||||||||||||||||||||||||||||||||||||||||

FOR THE RICE:
¾ cup pale ale
1 cup water
Pinch salt
1 cup white rice
2 tablespoons lime juice (about 1 large lime)
¼ cup minced cilantro
1 tablespoon olive oil
½ teaspoon salt

Slow-cooking chicken in a beer braise will give you a nice and tender, juicy bird. Put it on a bed of drunken cilantro lime rice and it's like Cinco de Mayo all year long.

1. In a large pot over medium-high heat, add the beer and the water; bring to a boil. As soon as the water boils, add the salt and rice and stir. Bring to a boil again, cover, and reduce heat to the lowest setting. Set timer for 18 minutes. Once the timer goes off, turn off heat and allow rice to sit for 4 minutes before lifting the lid.

2. While the rice is cooking, start cooking the onions and peppers: In a cast-iron skillet, over medium-high heat, add 2 tablespoons olive oil. Add the peppers and onions, sprinkle with ½ teaspoon salt, and cook until soft, about 10 minutes. Remove peppers and onions from pan.

3. In a small bowl, add 1 teaspoon salt, pepper, chipotle chili powder (or substitution), black pepper, garlic powder, and cumin. Stir to combine. Sprinkle the chicken with the spices and rub to coat.

4. Return the pan used to cook the onions and peppers to medium-high heat. Add additional oil if the pan has dried. Allow pan to get hot but not smoking. Sear the chicken on all sides until browned, about 3 minutes per side.

FOR THE PEPPERS AND CHICKEN:

2 tablespoons olive oil

2 red bell peppers, sliced (stem and
    seeds removed)

1 white onions, sliced

1 teaspoon salt

1 teaspoon pepper

2 teaspoons chipotle chili powder
    (or 1½ teaspoons chili powder and
    ¼ teaspoon smoked paprika)

1 teaspoon black pepper

1 teaspoon garlic powder

½ teaspoon cumin

4 boneless, skinless chicken thighs

2 cups pale ale

5. Pour beer over chicken until almost covered but not fully submerged. Loosely cover the pan, venting the lid to allow steam to escape, turn heat to low, and cook until chicken is cooked through, about 10 minutes.

6. Once the chicken is cooked, remove from pan and shred, using two forks.

7. Once the rice is finished, add the lime juice, cilantro, olive oil, and 1 teaspoon salt to the rice in the pan; toss to combine. Plate the rice, top with peppers and onions, and then top with chicken. Serve immediately.

Choose the Right Brew!

This chicken likes spice. Look for a pale ale, a blonde, or even a wheat beer that has a kick. More and more breweries are using peppers in their beers. If you can't find one, a pale ale with notes of citrus will do just fine.

Beer Marinara
TURKEY MEATBALL SANDWICHES

6 SANDWICHES

FOR THE SAUCE:
1 tablespoon olive oil
1 cup white onion, chopped
3 cloves garlic, peeled and minced
1 (28-weight ounce) can crushed
   tomatoes (3 cups)
3 tablespoons tomato paste
1 teaspoon salt
1 teaspoon fresh oregano, chopped
2 teaspoons chopped fresh basil
1 teaspoon crushed red pepper flakes
12 fluid ounces pale ale

It's just a sandwich. Okay, it's just the best meatball sandwich ever. That's all.

1. To make the sauce, in a large pot over medium-high heat add 1 tablespoon olive oil. Add 1 cup onions, and cook until softened. Add 3 cloves crushed garlic and stir. Add crushed tomatoes with their juices, tomato paste, salt, oregano, basil, red pepper flakes, and 12 ounces pale ale; reduce heat to medium-low to maintain a low simmer.

2. In a separate pan, start the meatballs by heating 1 tablespoon olive oil over medium-high heat. Cook the remaining ½ cup onions until softened, about 5 minutes. Add 1 clove minced garlic and cook for about 20 seconds. Remove from heat; add ¼ cup beer and stir. Pour onions, garlic, and beer into a large bowl, reserving pan.

3. Allow the onions and garlic to cool slightly. Then add the ground turkey, egg, cheese, rosemary, breadcrumbs, salt, and pepper to the bowl. Mix until just combined. Form mixture into meatballs just a bit smaller than golf balls.

4. Return pan used to cook the onions to medium-high heat, adding more oil if pan is dry, enough to just barely coat the bottom. Once the oil is very hot but not smoking, add the meatballs. Pull the pan back and forth across the burner, gently rolling the meatballs in the pan.

FOR THE MEATBALLS:

1 tablespoon olive oil
½ cup white onion, diced
1 clove garlic, peeled and minced
¼ cup pale ale
1¼ pounds ground turkey
1 large egg
¼ cup grated Parmesan cheese
1 teaspoon chopped fresh rosemary
1 cup dried Italian style breadcrumbs
½ teaspoon salt
1 teaspoon freshly ground black pepper

FOR THE SANDWICHES:

4 weight ounces provolone cheese, sliced
6 crusty Italian sandwich rolls

5. Once the meatballs have started to brown, add them to the pot of sauce. Raise the heat to bring sauce to a strong simmer and cook until the meatballs are cooked through and the sauce has thickened slightly, about 10 minutes.

6. Preheat oven broiler.

7. Slice the sandwich rolls and fill with meatballs and sauce. Top with cheese. Place under broiler just until the cheese has melted, about 2 minutes. Serve immediately.

Choose the Right Brew!

Looks for a pale ale with a medium-hop profile and notes of herbs to bring the right flavors to this sandwich. For a more intense beer taste, look for more hops; for a lower beer taste, grab one with less hops.

Brown Ale–Brined
ROAST TURKEY

SERVES 6–8

10 cups of water

2½ cups kosher or sea salt (do not use iodized table salt)

5 cloves garlic, quartered

¼ cup whole allspice berries

1 tablespoon whole cloves

2 large white onions, quartered

22 fluid ounces brown ale

2 cups ice

1 (12–16-pound) turkey (fresh works best; be sure to thaw it if frozen)

3 celery stalks, cut in half

¼ cup olive oil

Kosher or sea salt (for seasoning the turkey pre-oven)

2 cups chicken broth, plus 4–6 cups water if needed

This is a recipe I developed years ago for Thanksgiving, and it's become a steadfast tradition. Brining the turkey in brown ale creates the perfect bird: juicy, with a crispy skin with slight notes of malt. This recipe takes three days, so if this is the centerpiece of your Thanksgiving feast, plan to start the process on Tuesday night. If your turkey weighs more than 18 pounds, simply double the brine recipe. You'll need a couple of large turkey oven bags and a roasting pan with a rack.

1. In a large pot add the water, salt, garlic, allspice, cloves, and one of the onions.

2. Just as the water starts to boil, remove from heat, stirring occasionally to dissolve the salt. Add the beer and ice; stir. Cool to room temp, refrigerating if necessary. (If the brine is too hot, the turkey will start to cook, which can allow bacteria to grow.)

3. Rinse the turkey and remove any items from the cavity. Place one oven bag inside the other and then place the turkey inside those. Pour the brine over the turkey. Remove as much air as possible and tie bags to seal as tightly as possible. Place turkey bag on the roasting rack inside the roasting pan. Place in the refrigerator.

4. Brine for 16–18 hours. Rotate the turkey every 6–8 hours to ensure it marinates evenly. Remove from the brine and rinse, inside and out. Discard the brine and the bags.

5. Place turkey back on the roasting rack inside the roasting pan. Place in the fridge, uncovered, for 12–18 hours to dry the skin. (This will give you a nice crispy skin to go along with your juicy bird.)

6. Preheat oven to 400°F. Stuff the remaining quartered onion and the celery stalks inside the cavity of the bird. Truss turkey if desired. Brush the entire turkey with olive oil; sprinkle with salt.

7. Add the broth to the bottom of the roasting pan. If the pan starts to dry out as it roasts, add more water to the bottom of the pan. Do not allow the broth/water in the roasting pan to touch the turkey. Cook until your turkey reaches about 165°F, and then test the temperature with a meat thermometer inserted into the thickest part of the thigh (it will continue to cook and its internal temperature will continue to rise once it's out of the oven). Let rest for 10 minutes before carving.

Choose the Right Brew!

Look for a rich, nutty brown ale with notes of nuts, spices, and cloves. Select a low-hop profile; a high-hop profile will leave a slightly bitter taste.

Approximate Roasting Times Per Weight

8–12 pounds	2–3½ hours
12–16 pounds	3–4 hours
16–20 pounds	4–5 hours
20–25 pounds	5–6 hours
25–30 pounds	6+ hours

BROWN SUGAR AND BROWN ALE NIÇOISE
Chicken Thighs

SERVES 4–6

1 teaspoon salt
1 teaspoon pepper
3 tablespoons brown sugar, plus
   1 tablespoon divided
6 chicken thighs, bone in, with skin
3 tablespoons unsalted butter
1 tablespoon olive oil (plus additional
   if needed)
½ cup yellow onions, diced
2 cloves garlic, minced
⅔ cup Niçoise olives, pitted and sliced
   (pitted Kalamata olives can be
   substituted)
⅔ cup brown ale
1 cup chicken broth
12 prunes, pitted and diced
2 tablespoons oregano
¼ cup chopped flat-leaf parsley
Rice for serving

One of the first recipes I ever really fell in love with was Chicken Marbella from The Silver Palate Cookbook *by Julee Rosso and Sheila Lukins. The flavors are so well balanced and the chicken so moist, I keep going back to it. This recipe is a beer–ified version of that classic dish. Try it for a flavorful, one–pot, cast–iron skillet meal.*

1. In a small bowl combine the salt, pepper, and brown sugar, stirring to combine.

2. Sprinkle chicken on all sides with the seasoning mixture, rubbing and pressing sugar and spices into chicken.

3. In a cast-iron skillet over medium-high heat, add the butter and oil and heat until hot but not smoking. Add the chicken, searing until well browned on all sides, about 3 minutes per side. Remove from skillet and set aside.

4. Add the onions and sauté until soft, about 3 minutes. Use additional olive oil if the pan starts to dry. Add the garlic and stir for about 30 seconds.

5. Add the olives, beer, broth, and prunes. Cook until liquid has reduced by half, about 8 minutes.

6. Add the chicken back into the pan, sprinkle with oregano and remaining brown sugar, and cook until chicken has cooked through, about 20–25 minutes.

7. Just prior to serving, sprinkle with parsley. Serve over rice.

Choose the Right Brew!

A brown ale will give you a nice balance of hops to malt. Look for something with notes of nuts, honey, or spices. Stay away from anything that is too hop-forward.

Honey Mustard
PALE ALE CHICKEN

SERVES 4

1/3 cup Dijon mustard
1/4 cup honey
1/2 cup pale ale
2 tablespoons cornstarch
1/4 teaspoon salt
1/2 teaspoon pepper
1 clove garlic
2 tablespoons lemon juice
1 tablespoon unsalted butter
4 boneless, skinless chicken thighs
Salt and pepper
Rice for serving

Chicken thighs are starting to rise in popularity in North America. Where the chicken breast used to rule the roost, we are starting to wake up to what the rest of the world has known all along: The dark meat just has more flavor. Boneless, skinless chicken thighs are readily available at most commercial grocers, are often less expensive, and infinitely tastier. This cut is also simple to cook, not drying out as easily as that chicken breast fillet, making it a great choice when exploring cooking with the darker chicken meats.

1. Preheat oven to 375°F.

2. Add the mustard, honey, beer, cornstarch, 1/4 teaspoon salt, 1/2 teaspoon pepper, garlic, and lemon juice to a food processor, and process until smooth.

3. Melt butter in an oven-safe skillet over medium-high heat. Sprinkle chicken with salt and pepper on all sides. Sear chicken on both sides until browned.

4. Pour mustard sauce over chicken and bake at 375°F until chicken is cooked through, 22–25 minutes.

5. Plate chicken over rice; spoon desired amount of sauce over chicken.

Choose the Right Brew!

Look for a medium-hopped, citrusy American pale ale to find the right balance with the strong mustard notes in this recipe.

Beer-Brined
SALT-ROASTED CHICKEN

SERVES 4–6

2 tablespoons kosher or sea salt
16 fluid ounces brown ale
2 cups ice cubes
2½ cups cold chicken broth
4-pound whole roasting chicken
16 fluid ounces egg whites (about 10, to make 2 cups)
3 pounds kosher salt (about 7 cups)

Choose the Right Brew!

Brown ales often get overlooked when it comes to cooking, but this is where they can shine. Look for a brown ale with notes of nuts and spice to bring the right flavors to the chicken.

This recipe packs a double punch when it comes to delicious chicken. First, a beer brine gives you a juicy, well-tenderized bird, and then a salt crust encapsulates the entire chicken, steaming it in its own juices. Although you will have to sacrifice the skin, the superior meat is well worth it.

1. In a pot over medium-high heat, add 2 tablespoons salt and beer. Stir until salt has dissolved and beer is just starting to simmer; remove from heat. Stir in the ice cubes and broth to reduce temperature; set aside.

2. Rinse chicken, removing giblets from cavity if necessary.

3. Place chicken, breast side down, in a large bowl or small bucket, large enough to fit the chicken but small enough that the brine will cover the chicken.

4. Pour brine over chicken, cover, and refrigerate for 12–24 hours.

5. Preheat oven to 400°F.

6. Remove the chicken from brine, rinse well, and then truss.

7. In a large bowl, mix the egg whites and 3 pounds salt until well combined.

8. In a baking dish or roasting pan add about ¼ of the salt mixture, making a bed on which to set the chicken. Place chicken, breast side up, on the salt bed. Pack the remaining salt mixture over and around the chicken until fully encased.

9. Roast chicken at 400°F for 60–90 minutes or until the internal temperature reaches 165°F. (Press a thermometer through the salt pack and into the thickest part of the thigh to test temperature.)

10. Allow to rest for 5–10 minutes. Remove the salt and skin from the chicken. Move the chicken to a carving board to carve.

Note: To save yourself time, as well as wasted yolks, look for a 16-ounce carton of egg whites in your grocery store dairy case.

Paprika Chicken
WITH ROASTED RED PEPPER CREAM SAUCE [M]

SERVES 4

FOR THE CHICKEN:
- 1 cup IPA beer
- 1 cup chicken broth
- 1 tablespoon kosher salt, plus ¼ teaspoon, divided
- 3 pounds chicken parts, bone in, skin on (thighs, legs, wings)
- 1 tablespoon smoked paprika
- 1 teaspoon sweet paprika
- ½ teaspoon onion powder
- ¼ teaspoon nutmeg
- ⅛ teaspoon cayenne pepper
- 1 tablespoon olive oil

A few years ago I found myself in Fez, Morocco, unable to speak the language. The man who ran the hotel I was staying in took pity on me and walked me to his local neighborhood lunch spot. He introduced me to the owner, explained that I spoke only English, and asked that I be served the paprika chicken. Maybe it was the intensity of the situation, or maybe it was because it was my only option, but that was the best chicken I've ever had. I ate there every night, showing up hungry, using hand gestures to signify that I wanted the chicken again. Of all the things that happened that trip, the paprika chicken was one of my favorite parts. This is my version of a dish I'll never forget.

1. Add the beer, chicken broth, and salt to a large bowl; stir to combine. Add the chicken, and place bowl in the refrigerator for 3–6 hours. Remove chicken from the marinade; pat dry, discard the marinade.

2. Preheat oven to 425°F.

3. In a large bowl, mix together the smoked paprika, sweet paprika, onion powder, nutmeg, and cayenne. Add the chicken; toss until well coated. Allow to sit at room temperature for 10–15 minutes.

FOR THE SAUCE:

2 weight ounces cream cheese
2 tablespoons sour cream
2 tablespoons IPA
1 roasted red pepper
  (from a jar is fine)
¼ teaspoon salt
Rice for serving

4. Heat the olive oil in a large skillet. Add the chicken and brown before turning, about 4 minutes. Sear chicken on the other side, about 4 more minutes. Transfer to a 9" × 13" baking dish that has been lined with aluminum foil and place in the oven. Cook at 425°F for 30–35 minutes or until cooked through.

5. While the chicken is cooking, add all of the sauce ingredients to a food processor and process until smooth.

6. Plate chicken on top of rice, and cover with sauce prior to serving.

Choose the Right Brew!

Look for a citrusy IPA with notes of herbs to bring this chicken dish to life. You can use the same beer for both the sauce and the chicken. When you make the rice, you can even throw some into the cooking liquid for good measure!

Porter-Glazed
ASIAN CHICKEN MEATBALLS

MAKES 20 MEATBALLS

FOR THE MEATBALLS:
1 pound ground chicken (can substitute
   ground turkey)
1 cup panko breadcrumbs
¼ cup chopped green onion
½ teaspoon black pepper
½ teaspoon salt
½ teaspoon onion powder
½ teaspoon garlic powder
2 tablespoons porter
1 teaspoon fish sauce
1 large egg
2 tablespoons olive oil

With a sweet and sticky glaze, these meatballs can be skewered on toothpicks and served as an appetizer, or placed over rice as a meal. Although the beer flavor is slight in this dish, its malty notes give a nice finish to the spicy glaze.

1. In a large bowl, add all the meatball ingredients except the oil. Stir until just combined. Using a small cookie scoop or a tablespoon measuring spoon, form into small balls (the meatballs are best if bite-sized). Place on a plate that has been covered with a sheet of wax paper.

2. Place meatballs in the freezer for 15–20 minutes. This will help the meatballs keep their shape during cooking.

3. Add all glaze ingredients to a pot. Bring to a boil over high heat, stirring occasionally, until reduced and very thick and syrupy, 10–15 minutes. Cool to room temperature.

4. Heat 2 tablespoons olive oil in a skillet over medium-high heat until hot but not smoking. Add the meatballs, and pull the pan back and forth across the burner, rolling the meatballs around the pan. Cook meatballs until cooked through, about 10–12 minutes.

FOR THE GLAZE:

2 tablespoons honey
3 tablespoons golden brown sugar
¼ cup mirin
¼ cup soy sauce
½ cup porter
1 tablespoon red chili flakes
¼ teaspoon red chili sauce

5. Using a slotted spoon, transfer the meatballs to the glaze pan. Return glaze pan to low heat and roll around meatballs until well coated (if sauce is too cool, it will be too thick to cover meatballs). Remove meatballs to plate, and drizzle with remaining sauce. Skewer each meatball with toothpick or place over rice. Serve immediately.

Choose the Right Brew!

A strong, rich porter adds a kick of "meatiness" to the chicken and a malty flavor to the glaze.

STOUT AND CHEDDAR *Chicken Potpie*

SERVES 6

FOR THE FILLING:

3 tablespoons unsalted butter
1 cup white onion, chopped
2 ribs celery
3 carrots, peeled and sliced
1 red bell pepper, chopped, stem and seeds removed
3 boneless skinless chicken thighs, cut into bite-sized cubes
1 teaspoon salt
1 teaspoon pepper
2 tablespoons olive oil
¾ cup stout beer
⅔ cup corn kernels
½ cup peas
1 cup chicken broth
2 tablespoons all-purpose flour
8 weight ounces Cheddar, freshly grated
¼ cup heavy cream

FOR THE CRUST:

1 sheet puff pastry, thawed
Egg wash (1 large egg whisked with 1 tablespoon water)

Chicken potpie and good stout just seem to come from the same sensibility. On a cold day, a warm potpie and a rich stout will do you some good, or at the very least bring out the Irish side in you.

1. Preheat oven to 375°F.

2. In a large pot or skillet, melt the butter over medium-high heat. Add the vegetables and cook until softened, about 5 minutes.

3. Sprinkle chicken cubes on all sides with salt and pepper.

4. Add the oil to the pot, allowing to heat slightly before adding the chicken. Cook, stirring frequently, until the chicken is browned.

5. Add the stout, corn, peas, and chicken broth. Simmer, stirring occasionally, for about 10 minutes. Sprinkle with flour, and stir until combined.

6. Lower heat and whisk in cheese about ¼ cup at a time, allowing to fully combine before adding more. Remove from heat and slowly stir in cream.

7. On a lightly floured surface, roll puff pastry into a large rectangle. Cut into 6 equal-sized squares.

8. Place 6 individual-sized oven-safe bowls on a baking sheet.

9. Divide filling evenly between bowls. Top each bowl with a square of puff pastry; cut one or two small slits in the top of each pastry.

10. Brush pastry with egg wash. Cook until pasty has browned, 15–18 minutes.

Choose the Right Brew!

Find a stout with some notes of spice, smoke, or even nuts to bring an added depth to this big bowl of comfort.

WHITE BEAN AND BEER *Chicken Chili*

4 SERVINGS

3 boneless skinless chicken thighs
2 tablespoons unsalted butter
1 jalapeño, stemmed, seeded, and
  chopped
1 Pasilla (poblano) pepper, chopped
1 large white onion, chopped
¼ cup masa harina
1 (15-weight ounce) can butter beans,
  rinsed and drained
1 (15-weight ounce) can cannellini
  beans, rinsed and drained
2 cups chicken broth
12 fluid ounces pale ale
1 ear yellow corn, kernels cut off
  (¾ cup; if using frozen, thaw prior
  to use)
½ teaspoon garlic powder
½ teaspoon cumin
1 teaspoon salt
½ teaspoon black pepper
Pinch cayenne
¼ cup heavy cream
½ cup cilantro, chopped
2 large avocados, sliced

Warm and comforting but with an easy weeknight sensibility, this is a great go-to meal when you want something full of flavor and low on fuss. You can kick up the heat a bit, and even add some cheese and sour cream. Not only is this dish easy to tailor to your palate, it also works well with many different beer styles.

1. Boil the chicken over medium-high heat in pot of lightly salted water until cooked through. Remove from pot. Shred into bite-sized pieces using two forks.

2. In a large pot or Dutch oven, melt the butter. Add the jalapeño, Pasilla, and onion, and cook until peppers and onions have softened. Sprinkle with masa harina and stir to combine.

3. Add shredded chicken, both kinds of beans, broth, beer, corn kernels, garlic powder, cumin, salt, pepper, and cayenne. Simmer until thickened, about 10 minutes.

4. Remove from heat and stir in cream. Ladle into bowls; top with cilantro and avocado.

Choose the Right Brew!

Look for a pale ale with notes of herbs and citrus for this chili. The higher the hops the higher the beer bitterness will be. Keep that in mind when you reach for an IPA.

STOUT AND POMEGRANATE–GLAZED
Chicken Wings

4–6 APPETIZER-SIZED PORTIONS

2 pounds chicken wings
½ cup pomegranate juice
1 cup stout beer
¼ cup brown sugar
1 tablespoon soy sauce
1 teaspoon chili powder
1 teaspoon red chili flakes
1 tablespoon honey
2 tablespoons balsamic vinegar
1 teaspoon black pepper

Choose the Right Brew!

Grab a stout or a porter with notes of cherries or nuts to play nice with the pomegranate juice.

Chicken wings are always a good time when a game is on, and the party is at your place. Update your standard recipe with a sweet and sticky pomegranate stout glaze. Like a tuxedo t-shirt, it says, "I'm fancy, but I also like to party."

1. Preheat oven to 425°F.

2. Rinse the chicken wings; pat dry. Arrange evenly on a baking sheet covered with parchment paper or aluminum foil.

3. In a pot over medium-high heat, add the pomegranate juice, stout, brown sugar, soy sauce, chili powder, chili flakes, honey, balsamic vinegar, and black pepper. Bring to a boil, stirring frequently, until thick and syrupy, 10–15 minutes. Remove from heat.

4. Brush the chicken wings on all sides with the glaze.

5. Bake at 425°F for 10 minutes. Remove from oven and re-brush with glaze, flipping with tongs to brush both sides. Return to oven, cook for another 10 minutes, and then re-brush with glaze. Repeat this process until the chicken is cooked through. Total cooking time will be 20–30 minutes, depending on the size of the chicken wings.

Chapter 8

SEAFOOD

Beer and Butter Garlic Prawns ... 158

Beer-Brined Prosciutto–Wrapped Scallops
with Stout Balsamic Glaze ... 159

IPA Crab Cakes with Spicy Beer Hollandaise ... 162

Lobster, Corn, and Beer Chowder ... 165

IPA Watermelon Ceviche [H] ... 169

Pilsner Coconut Curry Shrimp Soup ... 171

Maple and Bourbon Barrel-Aged Beer–Glazed Salmon ... 172

Salmon with Dijon Beer Cream Sauce
over Drunken Couscous ... 174

Beer and Butter
GARLIC PRAWNS

SERVES 4

1½ pounds prawns, heads on
½ cup unsalted butter
2 tablespoons olive oil
8 cloves garlic, minced
1 teaspoon salt
1 teaspoon pepper
¾ cup blonde ale
1 large lemon
⅓ cups chopped flat-leaf parsley

I love this dish served in a cast-iron skillet to a group of hungry friends who don't mind rolling up their sleeves and getting their hands messy. Serve this with a nice crusty bread to sop up all of that great garlic butter sauce.

1. Using a sharp knife, slice down the back of the prawns and remove the vein. Rinse prawns and set aside.

2. In a large skillet melt the butter with the olive oil. Add the garlic and stir for about 20 seconds. Add the shrimp, salt, and pepper, and stir.

3. Pour beer over shrimp, and squeeze the juice from the lemon into the skillet.

4. Cook shrimp on both sides until pink and cooked through, 3–5 minutes per side. Garnish with chopped parsley. Serve immediately.

Choose the Right Brew!

Look for a crisp blonde or pale ale with low to medium hops and notes of citrus.

Beer-Brined
PROSCIUTTO–WRAPPED SCALLOPS WITH STOUT BALSAMIC GLAZE

8 SCALLOPS

FOR THE SCALLOPS:
1 cup room-temperature pale ale
2 tablespoons kosher or sea salt (do not use iodized table salt)
1 lemon, juiced
3 cups cold water
8 jumbo scallops
8 slices prosciutto
2 tablespoons unsalted butter

FOR THE BALSAMIC GLAZE:
⅓ cup stout beer
⅔ cup balsamic vinegar
1 tablespoon honey

Your everyday grocery store scallops will most likely come to you soaked in a phosphate solution that robs them of restaurant–quality greatness. The best way to tackle this is with a good brine. Beer is a natural tenderizer and will help to wash out that soapy taste and give you a high–end scallop flavor right at home.

1. In a large bowl, add the beer and salt and stir until the salt has mostly dissolved. Add the lemon juice and water and stir to combine.

2. Add the scallops to the brine; refrigerate for 30–45 minutes.

3. While scallops brine, make the glaze. In a saucepan over medium-high heat, add the stout, balsamic vinegar, and honey. Boil, stirring occasionally, until it has reduced and thickened, about 10 minutes. Remove from heat.

4. Remove scallops from brine and rinse well.

5. Place scallops on a stack of 3 or 4 paper towels; top with additional paper towels. Allow scallops to drain and dry at room temperature for about 10 minutes.

6. Fold the slices of prosciutto over lengthwise, making them just shorter than the height of the scallop.

(continued)

7. Tightly wrap each scallop; secure prosciutto with a toothpick.

8. In a large saucepan add the butter and melt over moderately high heat until it is hot but not browned.

9. Add the scallops to the pan and cook 3–4 minutes before turning (take care not to overcrowd the pan, as scallops will not brown; cook in batches if necessary).

10. Turn scallops and cook on the opposite side until scallops are cooked through, 3 additional minutes.

11. Drizzle scallops with glaze just prior to serving.

Choose the Right Brew!

You'll need two different beers for this recipe. For the scallops, look for a medium- to low-hopped pale ale with lots of citrus and floral notes. For the glaze, use a rich, bold stout with notes of oak, bourbon, or cherries. If you can find an oyster stout, all the better.

IPA CRAB CAKES WITH SPICY
Beer Hollandaise

MAKES 4 CRAB CAKES

You always have fun when you're eating crab cakes. Add beer and a spicy hollandaise and you just can't miss.

FOR THE CRAB CAKES:
8 weight ounces fresh lump crabmeat
1 large egg
2 tablespoons green onion, chopped
¼ cup roasted red peppers, chopped
¼ teaspoon salt
½ teaspoon pepper
½ teaspoon Old Bay seasoning
Pinch cayenne
2 tablespoons IPA beer
1 tablespoon melted unsalted butter
1 cup panko, plus 1 cup, divided
¼ cup canola oil

FOR THE HOLLANDAISE:
4 tablespoons butter
5 egg yolks
2 tablespoons lemon juice
2 tablespoons IPA beer
½ teaspoon red chili sauce (such as Sriracha)
Salt and pepper

1. To make the crab cakes, in a medium-sized bowl mix together the crabmeat, egg, green onions, red peppers, salt, pepper, Old Bay, cayenne, beer, melted butter, and 1 cup panko.

2. Form into 4 patties, about 1" thick. Place remaining panko in a small bowl. One at a time, place the patties in the panko and press until well coated on all sides.

3. In a pan over medium-high heat, add the canola oil. Cook crab cakes until golden brown on the underside. Flip carefully and cook on the other side until cooked through, about 3 minutes per side. Remove from heat.

4. To make the hollandaise, place 4 tablespoons butter in a microwaveable glass dish. Microwave on high for 45 seconds (or until melted); remove from microwave and let stand for 1 minute. Spoon off and discard the top layer of white foam.

5. In a large saucepan, add the yolks, lemon juice, and beer. Whisk quickly and continually over low heat until the mixture is frothy and doubled in size about 5 minutes. Keep heat low—too much heat will scramble the eggs.

(continued)

6. While continuing to whisk, slowly add the butter in a steady stream. Continue to whisk until thickened, 5–8 minutes. If your sauce gets too dry and thick, add a few teaspoons of water or beer. Add the chili sauce, and salt and pepper to taste.

7. Serve the crab cakes topped with hollandaise sauce.

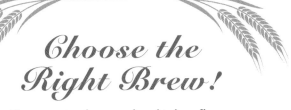

Choose the Right Brew!

This is a recipe that can take a big beer flavor. Grab an IPA that has citrus notes, but not too strong a malt taste, to give your crab cakes just the right flair.

LOBSTER, CORN, AND BEER
Chowder

SERVES 7

2 large raw lobster tails, thawed if frozen

2 ears corn

3 tablespoons unsalted butter

2 cups milk

1 cup cream

1 cup stock (fish or vegetable)

2 tablespoons olive oil

1 red bell pepper, chopped, stem and seeds removed

1 large yellow onion, chopped

1 cup red potatoes, peeled and diced

1 cup pilsner or blonde ale

¼ teaspoon smoked paprika

½ teaspoon salt

⅛ teaspoon cayenne

2 tablespoons clam juice (Note: Look for it in the market near the canned tuna.)

½ teaspoon black pepper

6 leaves basil, cut into thin ribbons

Even if you can't make it to a good ol' fashioned fish boil, lobsterfest, or clam bake this year, there's no reason you can't create some of those great flavors in your own kitchen. For those of us not so blessed as to reside in a lobster–rich region of the world, previously frozen raw lobster tails will do.

1. Remove the meat from the lobster tails; save shells and juices. Cut meat into chunks, place in a small bowl, cover tightly with plastic wrap, and refrigerate until ready to use. Add shells and juices to a stock pot.

2. Cut the corn off the ears, set corn aside, and add the cobs to the lobster tails in the stock pot.

3. Add the butter, milk, cream, and stock to the pot. Bring to a gentle simmer over medium-low heat (do not boil) and cook, stirring occasionally, for 30 minutes.

4. In a separate pot or Dutch oven, heat the olive oil. Add the bell pepper, onion, and potatoes, and sauté for about 5 minutes.

5. Add the corn, beer, paprika, salt, cayenne, clam juice, and black pepper.

6. Using a mesh sieve, strain the milk mixture into the Dutch oven, removing all pieces of shell and corn cob.

7. Simmer chowder until potatoes have softened, about 15 minutes.

8. Remove half of the soup (about 3 cups) and add to a blender or food processor; purée until smooth, then return to the stock pot. An immersion blender can be used, but take care not to purée all the ingredients; some texture from the chopped vegetables is desired.

9. Add the lobster and poach until cooked through, about 5 minutes. Sprinkle with basil just prior to serving.

Choose the Right Brew!

A pale ale, pilsner, or blonde ale with a low- to medium-hop profile and notes of citrus or herbs will be the best choice for this chowder. Stay away from anything that has too high a hop profile; the bitterness will be distracting.

IPA *Watermelon* CEVICHE [H]

SERVES 4

1 pound raw shrimp, peeled, deveined, and chopped
½ cup lime juice
½ cup lemon juice, plus ½ cup, divided
3 cups seedless watermelon, diced
½ cup red bell pepper, diced
⅓ cup white onion, diced
1 large jalapeño, stem and seeds removed, diced (about ¼ cup)
⅓ cup chopped cilantro
1 cup IPA beer
1 teaspoon kosher or sea salt
1 teaspoon red chili sauce
Tortilla chips for serving

This is what you want when the weather is so hot that you can't even think about turning on the oven. While the shrimp are "cooking" in the citrus juice, the watermelon is soaking up the flavors and goodness of your favorite high-hop beer. Because the beer isn't cooked, be careful whom you serve this to. The alcohol is still alive and well!

1. In a small bowl, add the chopped shrimp. Pour ½ cup lime juice and ½ cup lemon juice over the shrimp and toss to combine. Cover tightly with plastic wrap and refrigerate until shrimp have turned opaque, 1–3 hours.

2. In a separate bowl add the watermelon, bell pepper, onion, jalapeño, cilantro, beer, and remaining ½ cup lemon juice; toss to combine. Cover tightly with plastic wrap and refrigerate for at least 1 hour or until ready to use.

3. Once shrimp have "cooked" in the acid from the citrus, drain.

4. Drain the watermelon mixture and return to bowl. Add the drained shrimp, salt, and red chili sauce to the watermelon. Toss to combine and add additional salt if desired.

5. Serve chilled with tortilla chips.

Choose the Right Brew!

Because the beer isn't reduced in this recipe, it's a great place for hops.
A higher-hop beer, like an American IPA, with notes of herbs or pine
will give you the right punch for this dish.

Pilsner Coconut Curry
SHRIMP SOUP

SERVES 4

2 tablespoons sesame oil
1 large shallot, chopped (about ¼ cup)
1 red bell pepper, sliced julienne
1 cup pilsner or blonde-style beer
3 cups low-sodium chicken broth
2 (13½-fluid ounce) cans unsweetened
   coconut milk
1 tablespoon red curry paste
1 teaspoon fish sauce
1 tablespoon mirin
2 teaspoons white sugar
1 teaspoon lime juice
¼ teaspoon salt
¼ teaspoon cayenne pepper
24 large shrimp, peeled and deveined
4 weight ounces rice noodles
   (about 1 cup, broken)
6 basil leaves, thinly sliced
¼ cup green onions, chopped

This soup has a sophisticated simplicity. With a touch of beer and a quick cooking time, this might just be your new chicken noodle soup.

1. In a large pot over medium-high heat, add the sesame oil. Sautee the shallots and the bell peppers until soft, about 5 minutes.

2. Add the beer, scraping to deglaze the pan.

3. Add the chicken broth, coconut milk, curry paste, fish sauce, mirin, sugar, lime juice, salt, and cayenne; simmer for 5 minutes.

4. Add the shrimp and noodles. Stir until both are cooked, about 3 minutes. Sprinkle with basil and green onions. Serve immediately.

Choose the Right Brew!

Go for a crisp, clean pilsner, blonde, or pale ale with notes of citrus and a low- to medium-hop profile. A high-hop or high-malt beer will be a bit too distracting with the delicate flavors of shrimp.

Maple and Bourbon
BARREL-AGED BEER–GLAZED SALMON

SERVES 4

¼ cup ponzu sauce (Note: Look for this in the market near the soy sauce.)
¾ cup bourbon barrel–aged beer
3 cloves garlic, minced
1 tablespoon brown sugar
1 tablespoon maple syrup
1 teaspoon sesame oil
¼ teaspoon chili powder
1 tablespoon lime juice (about 1 large lime, juiced)
4 salmon fillets (4–6 weight ounces each)
Rice or pasta for serving

Bourbon barrel–aged beers might be my favorite of all beers. These ales are aged in bourbon barrels, soaking up those great flavors the previous tenant left behind. These are sipping beers—the bourbon flavor is beautifully present in the taste, and the ABV is almost always a bit higher than most brews. In this dish, the strong flavor of salmon stands up well to a stout–and–bourbon marinade, but make sure to save some of that great beer for drinking!

1. In a small bowl whisk together all ingredients except salmon and rice or pasta until well combined. Put in a large zip-top freezer bag.
2. Add the salmon and remove as much air as possible from the bag before sealing. Place in the refrigerator and marinate 1–2 hours, rotating at least once.
3. Preheat broiler. Remove the salmon from the bag and place fillets on a baking sheet prepared with cooking spray. Save marinade for next step.
4. Place the marinade in a pot over medium-high heat. Boil until reduced and thickened, stirring frequently, 8–10 minutes.

5. Brush the salmon with the marinade glaze.

6. Place salmon under broiler and cook until salmon flakes easily, about 6 minutes. Brush salmon with glaze several times during cooking (about every 2 minutes).

7. Serve over rice or pasta.

Choose the Right Brew!

A bourbon barrel–aged stout is the right beer for this. The bourbon flavors are important in getting the right notes in the final taste. These aren't beers that can be found in the common grocery store. Make a trip to a beer and wine store to find a beer that has been aged in bourbon barrels.

SALMON WITH DIJON
BEER CREAM SAUCE OVER
Drunken Couscous

|||||||||||||||||||||||||||||||||||||||||||||||||||||||||

FOR THE COUSCOUS:

1 cup chicken or vegetable broth
⅓ cup brown ale
2 tablespoons unsalted butter
1 cup pearl couscous
2 tablespoons chives
¼ cup almond slivers

FOR THE SALMON:

4 (3-weight ounce) salmon filets
1–2 teaspoons salt
1–2 teaspoons pepper
2 tablespoons olive oil

Salmon has an elegant feel, and a creamy sauce packed full of flavor gives it a heartiness that can rival a steak. Put it all on top of a drunken pearl couscous and there won't be any leftovers.

1. In a pot over medium-high heat, add the chicken broth and beer and bring to a boil. Add the butter and couscous, stir for about 2 minutes, cover, and turn off heat. Let sit until couscous has cooked through and all of the liquid has absorbed, about 10 minutes.

2. Once the couscous is cooked, add the chives and almonds and toss to combine. Put aside.

3. Sprinkle the salmon generously with salt and pepper.

4. In a pan over medium-high heat, add 2 tablespoons oil and heat until hot but not smoking. Swirl the pan to distribute the olive oil.

5. Add the salmon fillets and cook undisturbed until golden brown on the underside, 3–4 minutes. Carefully flip and cook until salmon is cooked through, about another 4 minutes.

6. Remove salmon from pan and set aside.

FOR THE SAUCE:

2 tablespoons olive oil
1 medium shallot, minced
2 cloves garlic, minced
½ cup brown ale
2 tablespoons Dijon mustard
½ cup chicken or vegetable broth
½ cup cream

7. To make the sauce, add the remaining 2 tablespoons oil and the shallots. Cook the shallots until softened, stirring occasionally, about 3 minutes. Add the garlic and stir.

8. Add the beer, deglazing the pan and scraping the bottom. Add the mustard and chicken broth. Cook until reduced slightly, about 6 minutes.

9. Remove from heat; stir in cream. Return to a simmer and cook until thickened, about 5–8 additional minutes.

10. Serve salmon on top of couscous. Drizzle generously with Dijon cream sauce.

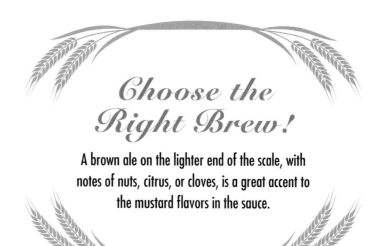

Choose the Right Brew!

A brown ale on the lighter end of the scale, with notes of nuts, citrus, or cloves, is a great accent to the mustard flavors in the sauce.

Chapter 9

DESSERTS

Amber Ale Carrot Cake with Orange Mascarpone Filling and
Beer-Spiked Cream Cheese Frosting [M] ... 179

Chocolate Porter Fudge Cookies ... 181

Chocolate Stout Brownies ... 182

Lemon Orange IPA Pudding with Beer Whipped Cream [M] ... 183

Chocolate Stout Cake with Chocolate Raspberry Ganache
and Whipped Cream [M] ... 184

Strawberry Pale Ale Popsicles [H] ... 187

Chocolate Stout Ice Cream with Pretzels ... 188

Chocolate Stout Mousse with Stout-Soaked Cherries [H] ... 190

Frosted Vanilla Beer Butter Cookies [M] ... 192

IPA Apple Fritters with Amber Ale Caramel Sauce ... 195

IPA Pavlova with Beer Lemon Curd, Strawberries, and
Beer Whipped Cream [M] ... 196

Lemon Pilsner Cheesecake with Beer Lemon Curd ... 198

Pale Ale Pastry Dough ... 201

Lime IPA Granita with Candied Basil [H] ... 203

Saison Caramelized Apple Cake with Beer Whipped Cream [M] ... 204

Tropical IPA Fruit Tart ... 206

Vegan Pumpkin Loaf Cake [M] ... 208

Chocolate-Chip Stout
Milk Shake [H] ... 209

Amber Ale Carrot Cake
WITH ORANGE MASCARPONE FILLING AND BEER-SPIKED CREAM CHEESE FROSTING [M]

SERVES 8–10

FOR THE CAKE:

1½ cups finely grated, peeled carrots (about 4 large carrots)
¼ cup unsalted butter
⅔ cup granulated white sugar
⅔ cup brown sugar
3 large eggs
1 cup amber ale
½ cup heavy cream
2 tablespoons canola oil
⅓ cup raisins
⅓ cup chopped pecans
2 cups all-purpose flour
2 teaspoons baking powder
1 teaspoon baking soda
1 teaspoon salt
1 teaspoon ground cinnamon
½ teaspoon ground nutmeg

Beer is a masterful ingredient when it comes to baking cakes. It gives this scrumptious dessert a texture so moist and light, your guests will forget there are vegetables in their cake.

1. Preheat oven to 350°F.

2. To make the cake, place the grated carrots on a stack of 3 or 4 paper towels and top with a similar stack. Press to remove moisture.

3. In the bowl of a stand mixer add ¼ cup butter, white sugar, and brown sugar; beat on high until well combined. Add the eggs, one at a time, mixing well and scraping the bottom of the bowl between additions.

4. Add the beer, cream, and oil. Mix, scraping the bottom of the bowl to ensure batter is fully combined.

5. Stir in the raisins, pecans, and shredded carrots.

6. In a separate bowl, add the flour, baking powder, baking soda, salt, cinnamon, and nutmeg ; whisk until well combined. Sprinkle the dry ingredients over the wet ingredients and stir gently until just combined.

7. Grease and flour two 9" cake pans. Divide the batter evenly between pans. Bake at 350°F until the top of the cake springs back when touched, 25–30 minutes. Allow to cool on a wire rack before removing cakes from the pans.

(continued)

FOR THE FILLING:

¼ cup (4 tablespoons unsalted butter, softened)
8 weight ounces mascarpone
2 tablespoons orange zest
1 cup powdered sugar
2 tablespoons amber ale

FOR THE FROSTING:

1 cup unsalted butter, softened
16 weight ounces cream cheese, softened
2½ cups powdered sugar
¼ cup amber ale

8. To make the filling, in the bowl of a stand mixer add ¼ cup softened butter and mascarpone. Beat on high until well combined. Add the orange zest, powdered sugar, and 2 tablespoons amber ale. Mix until well combined.

9. Spread the filling on the top of one layer of cake, and top with the remaining layer.

10. To make the frosting, in the bowl of a stand mixer, add 1 cup softened butter and cream cheese and beat on high until well combined. Add the powdered sugar and amber ale, and mix until well combined.

11. Frost cake with cream cheese frosting. Chill until ready to serve.

Choose the Right Brew!

An amber ale is a great choice, since they tend to have notes of caramel, cinnamon, and even nuts. If you can't find one you like, a nutty brown ale will work well also. Just stay away from a high-hop beer, opting for something a little more malty.

Chocolate PORTER FUDGE COOKIES

MAKES 20–24 COOKIES

8 weight ounces dark chocolate (60 percent), chopped, about 1¾ cups
⅓ cup stout beer
½ teaspoon vanilla extract
3 tablespoons butter
1 cup granulated sugar
3 large eggs
⅔ cup bread flour
2 tablespoons unsweetened cocoa powder
1 teaspoon espresso powder
¼ teaspoon baking powder
¼ teaspoon kosher salt
1 tablespoon cornstarch
1 cup semisweet chocolate chips
¼ teaspoon coarse sea salt

Choose the Right Brew!

This is no job for a pale ale. Reach for the deepest, darkest beer you can find! Look for a stout or a porter with notes of chocolate or espresso to bring out the richness in these cookies.

These are fantastic all on their own or as building blocks to other fabulous desserts. Fill them with ice cream for amazing ice cream sandwiches; add nuts or dried cherries to the batter for a little texture; or fill them with whipped cream for some unforgettable sandwich cookies.

1. In the top of a double boiler (or a metal bowl set over but not touching simmering water), add dark chocolate. Stir until melted and remove from heat. Stir in beer and the vanilla extract, then allow to cool to room temperature.

2. In the bowl of a stand mixer, add butter and sugar and beat on high until well creamed. Add eggs and mix on high until very light and fluffy, about 5 minutes. Add melted chocolate and beat until well combined, scraping the bowl to ensure the butter is fully incorporated.

3. In a separate bowl, add flour, cocoa powder, espresso powder, baking powder, kosher salt, and cornstarch. Stir until well combined.

4. Remove bowl from mixer, sprinkle with dry ingredients, and gently stir with a wooden spoon or spatula until just combined. Stir in the chocolate chips.

5. Cover the bowl and refrigerate until set, at least 30 minutes and up to 24 hours.

6. Preheat oven to 375°F.

7. Using a cookie scoop, drop about 1½ tablespoons of dough into mounds on a cookie sheet that has been covered with parchment paper. Sprinkle cookie balls with sea salt.

8. Bake cookies at 375°F for 12 minutes or until the top looks dry but the center is still soft. Don't over bake or the cookies will be dry. Cool until the center has set, about 20 minutes.

CHOCOLATE STOUT *Brownies*

18 BROWNIES

1½ cups unsalted butter, cut into cubes
10 weight ounces 60 percent chocolate, chopped (about 2 cups)
1 cup chocolate stout beer
1 teaspoon vanilla
4 large eggs
2½ cups white sugar
1 cup bread flour
2 teaspoons espresso powder
1 teaspoon salt
1 cup unsweetened cocoa powder
¾ cup semisweet chocolate chips

Choose the Right Brew!

It won't come as a shock when I tell you that this is the perfect recipe for a chocolate stout. Look for one made with real cocoa or chocolate to give a stronger and richer taste to these incredible treats.

Is there anything better than a rich brownie and a glass of stout? These are the perfect fudgy, gooey, you'll–need–a–napkin–and–probably–a–nap–afterward kind of brownie. They are perfect in a bowl topped with your favorite vanilla ice cream and served with a cold stout. This makes a big batch, so be prepared to share!

1. Preheat the oven to 400°F.

2. In the top of a double boiler (or a metal bowl set over but not touching simmering water), add the butter and the chocolate. Stir occasionally until just melted. Remove from heat and stir in the stout and vanilla.

3. In the bowl of a stand mixer beat the eggs on high until light and frothy, about 3 minutes. Add the sugar and beat for 8 full minutes.

4. In a separate bowl add the flour, espresso powder, salt, and cocoa powder; whisk until well combined.

5. Set mixture speed to low and add the chocolate mixture to the eggs. Mix until well incorporated, stopping to scrape the bottom of the bowl to ensure the batter is fully combined.

6. Remove the bowl from the stand mixer; sprinkle with remaining dry ingredients. Stir until just combined.

7. Grease a 9" × 13" baking dish, or spray with butter-flavored cooking spray. Pour in batter.

8. Place in the oven and immediately reduce to 350°F. Bake at 350°F for 40 minutes. The top of the brownies should look completely dry but the center should still be fudgy. Don't overbake. Remove from oven and cool to room temperature before cutting, about 1 hour.

Lemon Orange IPA PUDDING WITH BEER WHIPPED CREAM [M]

SERVES 4–6

FOR THE PUDDING:
¼ cup lemon juice (about 1 large lemon)
1 tablespoon lemon zest
¼ cup freshly squeezed orange juice (about 1 large navel orange)
1 tablespoon orange zest
½ cup IPA
2 tablespoons cornstarch
4 large egg yolks
1 cup cream
⅔ cup whole milk

FOR THE WHIPPED CREAM:
1 cup heavy cream
⅓ cup powdered sugar
2 tablespoons saison beer

Homemade pudding always reminds me of lazy summer days, good friends, and close family. Although homemade pudding is simple, it's a thoughtful, loving gesture that can be served with pound cake, fresh berries, shortbread, or all on its own.

1. Add all pudding ingredients into a pan (do not preheat pan). Place on stove and whisk continually over medium-high heat until thickened, about 10 minutes.

2. Pour into individual serving bowls; chill in fridge until set (about 4–6 hours).

3. Just prior to serving add all the whipped cream ingredients to a stand mixer and beat on high until soft peaks form, about 3 minutes.

4. Top with whipped cream before serving.

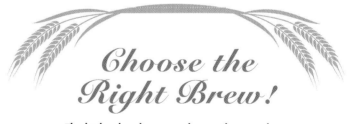

Choose the Right Brew!

The higher-hop beer you choose, the more beer flavor will come shining through. Look for one with citrus notes to set off the flavors of orange and lemon.

Chocolate Stout Cake WITH
CHOCOLATE RASPBERRY GANACHE
AND WHIPPED CREAM [M]

SERVES 15–18

FOR THE GANACHE:

20 ounces dark chocolate (60 percent cocoa), chopped, about 4 cups

1 cup chocolate stout

½ cup cream

1 cup fresh raspberries (plus additional for garnish, if desired)

FOR THE CAKE:

4 cups all-purpose flour

1 tablespoon baking powder

2 teaspoons baking soda

⅓ cup unsweetened cocoa powder

1 tablespoon espresso powder

½ teaspoon salt

1 cup (16 tablespoons) unsalted butter, softened

2⅔ cups granulated sugar

6 large eggs

8 weight ounces 60 percent dark chocolate, chopped (about 1¾ cups)

16 fluid ounces chocolate stout beer

¾ cup buttermilk

2 tablespoons vegetable oil

FOR THE WHIPPED CREAM:

4 cups (1 quart) heavy cream

1 cup powdered sugar

1 teaspoon vanilla extract

Once you bake a chocolate cake with a stout, you'll never want a sober cake again. Beer adds an amazing texture to any cake, but there is something extra special about a chocolate cake made with chocolate stout. You'll convert even a staunch teetotaler into a beer baker with this one. This makes a very large cake, so be prepared to share.

1. Start by making the ganache. In the top of a double boiler over medium heat (or a metal bowl set over but not touching simmering water), add the chocolate, beer, and cream. Stir until chocolate has melted and is well combined with the beer and cream.

2. Remove from heat and add the raspberries, stirring and breaking them up slightly. Place the bowl in the refrigerator and chill until the ganache has set to spreadable consistency, 2–4 hours.

3. Next, make the cake. Preheat oven to 350°F.

4. In a large bowl whisk together the flour, baking powder, baking soda, cocoa powder, espresso powder, and salt and set aside.

5. In the bowl of a stand mixer add the butter and sugar and mix on medium-high until well creamed.

6. One at a time add the eggs, stopping to scrape the bowl between additions.

7. In a microwave-safe bowl, microwave the chocolate and stout on high for 30 seconds. Stir and repeat until chocolate is melted.

8. Add the buttermilk, oil, and the chocolate mixture to the bowl of the stand mixer. Mix on medium until combined, stopping to scrape the bowl occasionally.

(continued)

9. Stop the mixer and sprinkle the dry ingredients on top of the wet ingredients. Gently mix on medium-low speed until just combined.

10. Grease and flour 3 10" cake pans liberally. (If you're using 9" pans, fill ⅔ full and use the remaining batter for cupcakes.) Divide the batter equally among the pans.

11. Bake at 350°F for 35–40 minutes or until the top springs back when touched. Cool the cake to room temperature on a wire rack before attempting to remove from the pan.

12. To assemble the cake, place one layer on a cake plate. Top with an even layer of about half of the ganache. Add a cake layer on top of the ganache. Spread evenly with the remaining ganache, and top with the remaining cake layer. Refrigerate until ready to frost with the whipped cream.

13. To make the whipped cream, add heavy cream, powdered sugar, and vanilla extract to the bowl of a stand mixer and beat on high until soft peaks form, 3–5 minutes.

14. Frost the entire cake with whipped cream. Refrigerate cake until ganache is fully set. Keep chilled until ready to serve. Top with additional raspberries, if desired.

Choose the Right Brew!

This needs a chocolate stout, and lucky for us, more and more breweries are adding them to their normal rotation. Look for a stout with notes of cocoa and espresso for this one.

STRAWBERRY PALE ALE
Popsicles [H]

8–10 POPSICLES

||||||||||||||||||||||||||||||||||||||||||||||||||||||||||||||||||||

2 cups chopped fresh strawberries
1 tablespoon water
1 cup sugar
1 tablespoon chopped fresh basil
   (2–4 large leaves)
3 tablespoons fresh lemon juice
1 cup IPA beer

You're always having fun when you're around boozy Popsicles! But be careful: These are Adults Only. Make sure to clearly label them when little ones are around.

1. In a pot over medium-high heat, add the strawberries, water, sugar, and basil. Bring to a simmer, stirring frequently, and cook until strawberries have broken down and turned syrupy, about 10 minutes. Cool slightly.

2. Add to a food processor with lemon juice and beer, and process until smooth.

3. Pour into Popsicle molds and freeze until set, 6–8 hours and up to 2 weeks.

Choose the Right Brew!

Because flavors dull once the temperature dips below 40°F, you want a bold beer that can still pack a punch once chilled. Look for a high-hop beer with citrus and even herb notes and a low ABV. Too high an alcohol content will make freezing a bit more difficult.

Chocolate Stout
ICE CREAM WITH PRETZELS

1 QUART

2 cups whole milk

1 cup cream

8 weight ounces 60 percent chocolate, chopped (about 1¾ cups)

1 cup chocolate stout

4 egg yolks

1½ cups sugar

1 cup mini pretzel twists, crushed

Choose the Right Brew!

Chocolate beer is where you go for this one. Either a porter or stout will do just fine, but look for something extra malty with lots of chocolate flavor.

What goes better with beer than pretzels? Now add beer into ice cream, America's favorite summertime treat, and you have a sweet-and-salty hit on your hands. And what about turning this into a milkshake with equal parts porter and milk? Just a thought.

1. In the top of a double boiler over gently simmering water (or a metal bowl set over but not touching simmering water), add the milk, cream, and chocolate. Stir until chocolate has melted. Remove from heat and cool for about 5 minutes.

2. In a large bowl, add the stout, egg yolks, and sugar. Whisk until well combined.

3. While continuing to whisk, slowly pour the hot chocolate mixture over the egg yolk mixture.

4. Return combined mixture to pot and stir over medium-high heat until it starts to thicken, about 5–8 minutes. If the mixture is lumpy, pour through a mesh strainer to remove lumps.

5. Transfer to a storage container, cover, and refrigerate until very cold, 6–12 hours.

6. Churn in ice cream maker according to manufacturer's specifications, adding the pretzels in the last 2 minutes of churn time (alternately, you can save the pretzels to use as a garnish for serving).

7. Transfer to a freezer-safe container. Freeze until firm, about 2 hours.

Note: Although the stout is cooked in this recipe, some alcohol may still be active. I would not recommend serving this to younger guests.

Chocolate Stout Mousse
WITH STOUT-SOAKED CHERRIES [H]

FOR THE MOUSSE:
1 cup heavy cream
¼ cup powdered sugar
2 tablespoons butter
1 (4-ounce) bar of dark chocolate
 (60 percent cocoa), chopped
 (about ⅔ cup)
1 teaspoon espresso powder
3 large room-temperature eggs,
 separated
⅓ cup chocolate stout beer
2 tablespoons granulated sugar

FOR THE CHERRIES:
12 sweet dark cherries (such as Bing),
 pitted
⅔ cup stout beer

This has a surprisingly light texture for something so full of beer, cream, and chocolate. That's just how I like it. Add in a couple of drunken cherries and you have yourself a party.

1. Whip the heavy cream and powdered sugar until soft peaks form. Chill until ready to use.

2. In the top of a double boiler (or a metal bowl set over but not touching simmering water), melt the butter. Add the chocolate and espresso powder; stir until just melted. Remove from heat and allow to cool until just above body temperature (about 100°F).

3. Place egg whites in one bowl and yolks in another large bowl.

4. Add ⅓ cup stout to the yolks, whisking until combined. Add the chocolate mixture to the egg yolks and whisk until combined.

5. Using a mixer, beat the egg whites until they are foamy and start to hold shape. While continuing to beat, slowly add in the 2 tablespoons granulated sugar and beat until soft peaks form, about 5 minutes.

6. Add half of the whipped cream to the chocolate mixture. Gently fold until incorporated. Add the whites, about ⅓ of the total whites at a time, gently folding until fully incorporated before adding more. Add the remaining whipped cream and gently fold in until just combined.

7. Add mousse to individual serving bowls (6–8 depending on size) and chill for at least 6 hours and up to 36.

8. Add cherries to a small bowl. Pour stout over cherries until submerged. Allow to sit at room temperature for 2–4 hours. Drain. Cover and chill prior to serving.

9. Top mousse with cherries prior to serving.

Note: This recipe contains raw eggs which can cause food-borne illnesses. To reduce these risks, use the freshest, highest quality eggs available, or look for raw, prepasteurized whole eggs for this recipe.

Choose the Right Brew!

This needs a strong dark beer. Look for an imperial stout with notes of chocolate or coffee to grab the right amount of beer flavor.

Frosted Vanilla
BEER BUTTER COOKIES [M]

MAKES 32 COOKIES

FOR THE COOKIES:
1 cup unsalted butter, softened
2 cups sugar
1 teaspoon vanilla
¼ teaspoon lemon extract
2 large eggs
½ cup heavy cream
½ cup beer (pale ale, amber ale, or wheat beer)
4½ cups all-purpose flour
Pinch of salt
1 tablespoon cornstarch
2 tablespoons baking powder
2 teaspoons baking soda

FOR THE FROSTING:
1½ cups butter, softened
3 cups powdered sugar
½ cup whole milk
¼ cup amber ale

Soft and delicate, just a hint of beer in the cookies and frosting makes these quite the vixens of the baked goods world. You can make the dough up to 36 hours ahead of baking—and your cookie exchange will never be the same.

1. To make the cookies, in the bowl of a stand mixer fitted with a paddle, add 1 cup softened butter and sugar and beat on medium-high until well combined. Reduce speed to medium, add the vanilla, lemon extract, and eggs, one at a time, and beat well between each addition, scraping the bottom occasionally.

2. Add the heavy cream and the beer; mix until incorporated.

3. Add the flour, salt, cornstarch, baking powder, and baking soda to a separate bowl, mix until combined, and then sprinkle dry ingredients on top of the ingredients in the mixer.

4. Stir gently with a spatula or wooden spoon until just combined, scraping the bottom to ensure the butter is fully incorporated.

5. Cover the bowl tightly and refrigerate for at least 3 hours and up to 36.

6. Scrape dough out of bowl onto a well-floured surface. Pat into a rectangle and dust the top with more flour.

7. Using a rolling pin, roll dough into an even ½"–¾" thickness. Using a large, round biscuit cutter, cut out cookies and place on a baking sheet that has been covered with parchment paper.

8. Place baking sheets in the refrigerator about 15 minutes.

9. Preheat oven to 325°F.

10. Bake cookies at 325°F for 12 minutes or until cookies have puffed and no longer look wet. Do not brown cookies. Immediately slide the parchment off the baking sheet and onto a flat surface.

11. To make the frosting, add the butter to the bowl of a stand mixer. Beat on high until light and fluffy. Add the powdered sugar and beat on low until mostly incorporated. Turn mixer to high and beat until light and fluffy. Slowly add the milk and beer; beat again until fully incorporated.

12. Allow cookies to cool prior to frosting.

Choose the Right Brew!

You have some options with this one. An amber ale will give you great notes of caramel and even some spice. But you can also reach for a wheat beer for bready notes or even a crisp pilsner.

IPA APPLE FRITTERS WITH
Amber Ale Caramel Sauce

32–38 FRITTERS

1½ cups cake flour
⅓ cup granulated sugar
2 tablespoons brown sugar
1 teaspoon baking powder
¼ teaspoon salt
1 teaspoon cinnamon
¼ teaspoon nutmeg
½ teaspoon vanilla
1 egg
½ cup IPA beer
2 cups Granny Smith apples, peeled,
   cored, and chopped (1–2 large)
Peanut or canola oil for frying
¼ cup powdered sugar
1 batch Amber Ale Caramel Sauce
   (Chapter 3)

These are best bite–sized. Make sure to keep them small in order to get the right golden brown on the outside and a fully cooked fritter on the inside. If these little treats are too large, you run the risk of a doughy center.

1. In a large bowl, mix together the flour, granulated sugar, brown sugar, baking powder, salt, cinnamon, and nutmeg.

2. In a separate bowl mix the vanilla, egg, and beer; whisk until combined. Add the wet ingredients to the dry ingredients and stir until just incorporated.

3. Gently fold in apples.

4. Add about 6 inches of oil to a pot and heat over high heat to 365°F using a deep-fry thermometer clipped to the pot. Adjust heat to maintain a temperature of 365°F.

5. Using a tablespoon measuring spoon, drop a rounded tablespoon of batter into the hot oil. Only fry 2–3 fritters at a time. Once the underside of the fritter is golden brown, flip with a heat-safe spatula or spoon. Cook on the other side until cooked through, 45–60 seconds per side.

6. Remove from oil and allow to drain on paper towels. Dust with powdered sugar. Serve with Amber Ale Dipping Sauce.

Choose the Right Brew!

An amber ale with notes of cinnamon or caramel is great for this. Look for a beer with lots of carbonation to lighten up the batter.

IPA PAVLOVA WITH
BEER LEMON CURD, STRAWBERRIES, AND
Beer Whipped Cream [M]

SERVES 8

FOR THE PAVLOVAS:
- 1 cup fine granulated sugar (such as castor sugar)
- 1 tablespoon cornstarch
- 3 large egg whites, room temperature (reserve the yolks for the lemon curd)
- Pinch salt
- 3 tablespoons cold flat IPA
- 1 teaspoon white vinegar
- ½ teaspoon vanilla extract

FOR THE CURD:
- 2 teaspoons lemon zest
- ½ cup fresh squeezed lemon juice (about 3 large lemons)
- ¼ cup IPA beer
- ¾ cup white sugar
- 1 tablespoon cornstarch
- 1 whole large egg plus 3 yolks
- ¼ cup unsalted butter, cut into cubes

Pavlovas are a great choice when entertaining. Easy, elegant, and oh so impressive. The curd and whipped cream can both be made ahead, and the pavlovas can be made earlier in the day. Just assemble, serve, sit back, and enjoy the lavish praise.

1. Preheat oven to 275°F.

2. To make the pavlovas, in a small bowl whisk together the sugar and 1 tablespoon cornstarch.

3. In the bowl of a stand mixer, add the egg whites and pinch of salt. Beat on medium speed until soft peaks form. While the mixer is running, slowly add the beer (meringue may loosen). Continue to beat whites until soft peaks return.

4. Turn mixer to high and slowly add the sugar mixture. Continue to beat until peaks start to firm up, 1–2 minutes. Slowly add the vinegar and vanilla, beating until stiff peaks form and meringue is glossy.

5. Cover a large baking sheet with parchment paper. Spoon meringue onto parchment in 8 equal-sized "nests," making an indentation in each round with a spatula. Each nest should be about 4" across, 2" high, and have a well in the center to hold the curd, fruit, and whipped cream.

6. Place baking sheet in the oven and bake until the miniature pavlovas are dry and "crisp" on the outside, 40–50 minutes. Turn off the oven, open the oven door halfway, and allow the pavlovas to cool in the oven until room temperature before removing.

FOR THE WHIPPED CREAM:
1 cup heavy cream
⅓ cup powdered sugar
2 tablespoons pale ale beer
1½ cups fresh strawberries, sliced

7. To make the curd, add the lemon zest, lemon juice, beer, sugar, 1 tablespoon cornstarch, whole egg, and yolks to a bowl; whisk until well combined. Add the lemon mixture to a pan over medium-low heat along with the butter. Whisk until thickened, about 10 minutes. Allow to cool to room temperature and then refrigerate until ready to use. (Curd can be made up to 3 days in advance; store in an airtight container in the refrigerator until ready to use.)

8. To make the whipped cream, in the bowl of a stand mixer add the cream, powdered sugar, and beer. Beat on high until soft peaks form, about 3 minutes.

9. Top each pavlova with lemon curd, then with diced strawberries, and finally with whipped cream before serving.

Choose the Right Brew!

A relatively small amount of beer is called for in this recipe, so grab one that packs a punch. Go for an American IPA with herb, citrus, or floral notes.

Lemon Pilsner Cheesecake
WITH BEER LEMON CURD

SERVES 12

FOR THE CRUST:
9 standard-sized graham crackers
2 tablespoons brown sugar
¼ teaspoon salt
3 tablespoons melted butter

FOR THE CHEESECAKE FILLING:
16 weight ounces cream cheese
1½ cups sugar
2 eggs
½ cup sour cream
¼ cup lemon juice
1 tablespoon zest
½ cup pilsner beer
3 tablespoons flour
2 tablespoons cornstarch

FOR THE CURD:
1 tablespoon lemon zest
½ cup freshly squeezed lemon juice
   (about 3 large lemons)
¼ cup pilsner
¾ cup white sugar
1 tablespoon cornstarch
1 whole large egg plus 3 large yolks
¼ cup unsalted butter, cut into cubes

This addictive little cheesecake is just about as creamy and light as you can get for something packed with beer and cream cheese. A soft aftertaste of beer keeps you coming back for more, and that lemon topping is the stuff that dreams are made of.

1. To make the crust, in a food processor add the graham crackers, brown sugar, and salt. Process until it's the consistency of crumbs. While the food processor is running, slowly add the butter and process until it resembles wet sand.
2. Spray the inside of a 9" springform pan with butter-flavored cooking spray. Pour the crust into the springform pan. Using the bottom of a heavy, flat-bottomed glass, press the crust into the bottom of the pan until well compacted.
3. To make the filling, in the bowl of a stand mixer add the cream cheese and the sugar and mix until smooth.
4. One at a time, add the eggs, scraping the bottom of the bowl between additions.
5. Add the sour cream, lemon juice, zest, and beer; stir until well combined.
6. Sprinkle with flour and cornstarch and stir until well combined.
7. Pour the batter into the pan over the crust; smooth out into an even layer.

(continued)

8. Place oven rack in the middle position. Preheat oven to 350°F.

9. Bake the cheesecake until puffed and the center only slightly jiggles when you shake the rack, about 50–60 minutes. The cheesecake will continue to set as it cools. Remove from oven; allow to cool slightly (about 10 minutes) before placing in the refrigerator.

10. To make the curd, add the lemon zest, lemon juice, beer, sugar, cornstarch, whole egg, and yolks to a bowl and whisk until well combined. Add the lemon mixture to a pan over medium-low heat, along with the butter. Whisk until thickened, 10–12 minutes. Cool to room temperature.

11. Pour curd over cheesecake; refrigerate until set, at least 4 hours and up to 24.

Choose the Right Brew

A clean crisp pilsner with notes of lemon is a great beer to grab for this creamy dessert. Too much malt can be a bit distracting, but if you want to pack on the beer flavor, you can roll the beer-flavored dice with a higher-hop brew.

Pale Ale PASTRY DOUGH

1 PIE CRUST

1½ cups flour, divided
½ teaspoon salt
1 tablespoon sugar
½ cup unsalted butter (or vegetable shortening), cut into cubes
¼ cup pilsner or wheat beer

Beer adds a tender texture to your average pastry dough, and because the alcohol cooks off, this crust has extra flakiness. This makes enough pastry for one pie crust or tart. For a double-crust pie, double the recipe.

1. In a food processor, add 1 cup of flour (reserving the other ½ cup), salt, and sugar; pulse to combine. Add the butter or shortening cubes; process until combined. Add the remaining ½ cup of flour; process until well incorporated.

2. Transfer from the food processor to a bowl. Add the beer and mix until combined. Dough will be very soft.

3. Form dough into a wide flat disk, wrap in plastic wrap, and chill for at least 2 hours.

4. On lightly floured surface, roll dough into an even circle, transfer to a pie pan, and process with your favorite pie recipe.

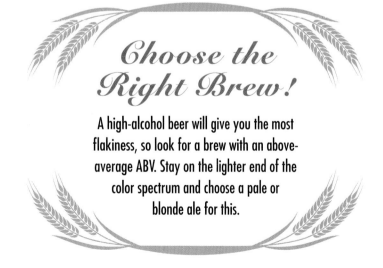

Choose the Right Brew!

A high-alcohol beer will give you the most flakiness, so look for a brew with an above-average ABV. Stay on the lighter end of the color spectrum and choose a pale or blonde ale for this.

LIME IPA *Granita* WITH CANDIED BASIL [H]

SERVES 4–6

FOR THE GRANITA:
½ cup water
1 cup sugar
12 fluid ounces IPA
½ cup lime juice
½ teaspoon lime zest

FOR THE BASIL:
½ cup sugar
3 tablespoons water
8 small basil leaves (each about
    1" in length)

Choose the Right Brew!

A high-hop beer with notes of citrus is what you want to grab for this frosty treat. Look for an IPA with the flavors of lemon and lime to complement this dish.

Granitas are a great way to serve up a summer treat when you don't have access to an ice cream maker. The candied basil gives this dish a fun and elegant twist that makes it fit for a swanky summer dinner party.

1. In a saucepan over medium-high heat, add ½ cup water and 1 cup sugar, stirring until sugar has dissolved completely. Remove from heat.

2. Add the beer, lime juice, and lime zest; stir to combine.

3. Pour into a 9" × 13" baking dish. Place in the freezer for 1 hour. Using a fork, scrape the mixture and break up the forming ice crystals.

4. Scrape every 30–45 minutes until mixture is mostly frozen, about 3 hours.

5. While granita is freezing, make the basil. Heat oven to 200°F.

6. In a pot over medium-high heat, combine ½ cup sugar and 3 tablespoons water. Stir until sugar has just dissolved; remove from heat and cool for 10 minutes.

7. Place basil leaves in the sugar water until fully coated. One at a time remove basil leaves, allowing most of the sugar water to drip off.

8. Place on a baking sheet that has been covered with parchment paper or a silicone baking mat. Bake for 15–20 minutes or until the sugar has crystallized. Gently flip the leaves and bake until the other side has crystallized, about 15 minutes. Remove from oven and cool.

9. Scoop granita into individual serving bowls and top with candied basil. Serve immediately.

SAISON CARAMELIZED *Apple Cake* WITH BEER WHIPPED CREAM [M]

SERVES 6–8

FOR THE APPLES:
¼ cup unsalted butter
⅔ cup brown sugar
¼ cup saison beer
2 large Granny Smith apples, cored, peeled, and thinly sliced

FOR THE CAKE:
1½ cups flour
1 teaspoon baking powder
½ teaspoon baking soda
½ teaspoon salt
1 teaspoon cinnamon
¼ teaspoon nutmeg
½ cup unsalted butter
½ cup white sugar
⅔ cup brown sugar
2 large eggs
1 teaspoon vanilla
⅓ cup buttermilk
½ cup saison beer
2 tablespoons vegetable oil

FOR THE WHIPPED CREAM:
1 cup heavy cream
⅓ cup powdered sugar
2 tablespoons saison beer

Saisons are summer beers, and most apples actually come into season during the late summer months. This is an easy cake to whip up for a late–summer dinner party on the patio. Serve a bubbly saison and celebrate the end of the season.

1. Preheat oven to 350°F.

2. To make the apples, in a pan over medium-high heat, add the butter, ⅔ cup brown sugar, and ¼ cup beer. Bring to a boil, stirring frequently. Add the apples and boil until reduced and thickened, about 12 minutes.

3. Lightly spray a deep-dish 9½" pie pan with cooking spray. Pour the apples with sauce into the pan.

4. To make the cake, in a large bowl whisk together the flour, baking powder, baking soda, salt, cinnamon, and nutmeg. Set aside.

5. In the bowl of a stand mixer, add the butter, white sugar, and brown sugar. Beat on high until well creamed. One at a time add the eggs and vanilla, scraping the bowl between each addition.

6. Add the buttermilk, ½ cup beer, and oil; mix on medium speed until well combined. Sprinkle the flour mixture over the bowl, and stir on medium-low speed until just combined, about 3 minutes. Pour the batter over the apples in an even layer.

7. Bake at 350°F for 35–40 minutes or until a toothpick inserted in the center comes out clean. Cool for about 10 minutes.

8. Invert the pie pan onto a serving plate.

9. To make the whipped cream, in the bowl of a stand mixer add the cream, powdered sugar, and 2 tablespoons beer. Beat on high until soft peaks form, about 3 minutes.
10. Serve cake warm, topped with whipped cream.

Choose the Right Brew!

Saisons are an often overlooked beer style, but their citrus notes and high carbonation levels make them a great choice for an apple cake. If you can't find a saison, look for a beer with notes of cinnamon, nutmeg, or citrus that has lots of great bubbles to lighten up that cake.

Tropical IPA FRUIT TART

SERVES 6

||||||||||||||||||||||||||||||||||||||||||||||||||||||||||||||||||||||||

FOR THE CRUST:
1 cup flour plus ½ cup, divided
½ teaspoon salt
1 tablespoon sugar
½ cup unsalted butter, cut into cubes
¼ cup pale ale or wheat beer

FOR THE CUSTARD:
1 cup heavy cream
½ cup IPA
⅔ cup sugar
2 large eggs, plus 2 extra yolks
2 tablespoons cornstarch
½ teaspoon salt
2 teaspoons vanilla extract

Although this recipe might seem a bit daunting, it's actually fairly simple. Better yet, this mouth-watering tart can be made up to a day ahead. Garnish tart just prior to serving or the almonds and coconut will become soft. A great choice for a summer gathering, or even a cold winter day when you just want a reminder of the warm tropics.

1. To make the crust, in a food processor add 1 cup of flour, salt, and sugar; pulse to combine. Add the butter cubes and process until combined. Add the remaining ½ cup of flour, and process until well incorporated.

2. Transfer mixture from food processor to a bowl. Add ¼ cup of beer and mix with a wooden spoon until combined. Dough will be very soft.

3. Form dough into a wide flat disk, wrap in plastic wrap, and chill for at least 2 hours.

4. Preheat oven to 350°F. On lightly floured surface, roll dough into an even circle. Transfer dough to a 9" tart pan with a removable bottom (or a 9" pie pan), press into shape, and remove excess dough. Prick the bottom several times with a fork, and line bottom with pie weights or dried beans. Bake at 350°F for 16–18 minutes or until light golden brown. Remove from oven and allow to cool before removing pie weights or beans.

5. To make the custard, in a saucepan over medium heat, bring the cream to a slight simmer, stirring occasionally. Remove from heat when bubbles start to form around the edges and cool slightly.

1½ cups diced mango, peeled and
   chopped (about 1 large mango)
1½ cups diced fresh pineapple
½ cup sugar
1 tablespoon butter
¼ cup IPA

FOR THE GARNISH:
½ cup sweetened coconut flakes
¼ cup sliced almonds

6. In a large bowl add ½ cup IPA, ⅔ cup sugar, eggs, yolks, cornstarch, ½ teaspoon salt, and vanilla; whisk until well combined. Very slowly whisk the cream into the egg mixture.

7. Return mixture to the pan and whisk over medium-high heat until thickened, 6–8 minutes. Cool slightly.

8. Pour custard into pie shell. Refrigerate until set slightly, about 30 minutes.

9. To make the topping, in a saucepan add the mango, pineapple, ½ cup sugar, 1 tablespoon butter, and ¼ cup IPA. Bring to a boil, stirring frequently, until very thick, 12–15 minutes. It should look like there isn't anything left in the pan but fruit and bubbles. Cool and then spread topping evenly over custard. Refrigerate until cooled and set, about 3 hours and up to 24. To make the garnish, add the coconut flakes and almonds to a dry pan over medium-high heat. Toss or stir until slightly browned, about 5 minutes. Top tart with toasted coconut and almonds. Coconut and almonds can be made up to 1 day ahead of time and stored in a separate airtight bag or container.

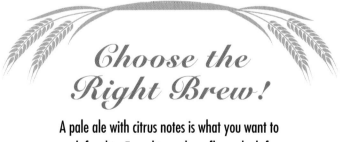

Choose the Right Brew!

A pale ale with citrus notes is what you want to grab for this. For a bigger beer flavor, look for a higher-hop beer, like an IPA; for a more mellow flavor, grab a pilsner or a lower-hop pale ale.

Vegan PUMPKIN LOAF CAKE [M]

SERVES 8–10

1¾ cups all-purpose flour
1 teaspoon cinnamon
¼ teaspoon nutmeg
1 teaspoon baking soda
1 tablespoon baking powder
1 cup dark brown sugar
½ cup white sugar
½ cup chopped pecans
1 teaspoon salt
1 (15-weight ounce) can pumpkin purée
1 teaspoon vanilla extract
2 tablespoons canola oil
⅔ cup pumpkin ale, plus 1 tablespoon, divided
1 (14-fluid ounce) unshaken can full-fat, unsweetened coconut milk
1 cup confectioners' sugar

Choose the Right Brew!

This cake lends itself to many different beer styles. A pumpkin ale is a great choice. A porter or a stout will give a maltier quality, and a pale ale will add a touch of acid.

This loaf cake is so rich and moist you'll never miss the eggs or dairy. The beer is used as a leavening agent and gives a great texture to this cake. Although I like to bake this in a loaf pan, you can use a traditional round pan or even muffin tins.

1. Preheat oven to 350°F.

2. In a large bowl, add the flour, cinnamon, nutmeg, baking soda, baking powder, brown sugar, white sugar, pecans, and salt. Stir to combine.

3. In a separate bowl add the pumpkin, vanilla extract, oil, and ⅔ cup beer. Remove the top of the coconut milk can without shaking. Scrape off ½ cup of fat, and reserve the rest of the can. Add the coconut fat to the bowl with the wet ingredients. Stir until well combined.

4. Add the wet ingredients to the dry ingredients and stir until just combined.

5. Spray a 1½-quart loaf pan with cooking spray. Pour batter into the prepared pan. Bake at 350°F for 60–65 minutes or until a toothpick inserted in the center comes out clean.

6. To make the icing, add 1 cup of confectioners' sugar and 1 tablespoon beer to a bowl.

7. Place contents of can of coconut milk in a separate bowl and stir until the milk and the fat have incorporated. Add 1 tablespoon of this coconut milk to the icing bowl. Stir until combined.

8. Pour icing over cooled cake. (Refrigerate for 30 minutes to set the icing, if desired.) Slice to serve.

CHOCOLATE-CHIP STOUT
Milk Shake [H]

SERVES 2

3 cups vanilla ice cream
1 cup dark chocolate chips
1 cup chocolate stout

Here an old-fashioned malt shop treat meets a pub favorite. The cold ice cream makes this a great dessert for summer, but the rich stout lets you know you can drink it all year long.

1. Add all ingredients to a blender. Blend until combined.
2. Serve immediately.

Choose the Right Brew!

A chocolate stout, of course! If you want to mix it up a bit, you can try a bourbon barrel aged–stout or for a new twist even a smoky porter.

Appendix

GLOSSARY of BEER TERMS

abbey, abbaye, abdj bier. For many years this meant a beer was made in an abbey or by monks. However, today it means that the beer is made in the Trappist tradition.

Adam's ale. Water; another way of calling a beer watery or weak.

additives. Preservatives that some brewers sometimes add in order to lengthen shelf life or enzymes that produce an artificial head, to give their beer the appearance of having body. Mostly found in beers manufactured by larger brewers.

adjuncts. Adjuncts are added to the barley malt during brewing. This is done to create certain effects. Crafters use wheat and oats to gain special flavors. Many larger manufacturers add corn as a cheap substitute, or as a way to make their barley go a little further.

alcohol. Alcohol results in beer as part of the traditional brewing methods through the fermentation of grains. A beer does not have to contain alcohol to be called beer. Most beers contain 4 to 5 percent alcohol.

ale. A beer made with top-fermenting yeast, usually characterized by a fruitiness of flavor. Ales do not take much time to create from brewing to serving. A lager, for example, needs to be stored before serving, while an ale does not. According to some state laws, ale denotes a higher alcoholic content than a lager. The world brewing community does not see it this way. Ales range from bitter to sweet and vary greatly in their alcoholic content.

aleberry (alebrew, albrey, alebery). A spiced ale, dating from the Renaissance, that was brewed with sugar, spice, and bits of bread.

ale-conner. In England, an inspector of ale. Shakespeare's father was an ale-conner.

alecy. A description of madness thought to be induced by beer.

alegar. Malt vinegar.

all barley. A beer brewed from only barley malt, with no other adjuncts, additives, grains, corn, rice, or sugars.

all malt. A beer brewed from only malted grains, with no other adjuncts, additives, corn, rice, or sugars.

alt. "Old" in German, as in *altbier*, meaning "old beer."

altbier. "Old beer" in German; this is the type of brewing that preceded lagers.

barley. The central ingredient to brewing beer. By placing mature barley in a kiln and firing it, malt is created, which helps give beer its flavor and color.

barley wine. Not really a wine at all, but a very strong ale with alcohol usually twice that of strong beers. Barley wine is brewed in colorations ranging from pale to dark. The term is English, coming from the fact that its alcohol content was closer to that of wine.

barrel. One barrel equals thirty-one U.S. gallons of beer. Usually used to measure a brewery's output.

Bayriche. German for Bavarian.

beer. Any drink made from fermented grains and, more than likely, hops. *Beer* is the generic term for an entire family of beverages. Ales, lagers, porters, and stouts are all considered beer. In America, beer is usually meant to be lager, while the English tend to mean ale when they ask for a beer.

Belgian lace. The residue left on the inside of a glass after the head expires. Belgium has been famous for centuries for both its beers and its lace.

Berliner weisse. Also known as wheat beer. Known for its low alcoholic content, this is a milky, white-ish beer that is highly carbonated.

bier. German for "beer."

bière ordinaire. French for "house beer."

bière de garde. A strong ale from France. Meant to be laid down or cellared.

bierworst. A German sausage flavored heavily with garlic. Usually dark.

bitter. An English ale brewed with high hop content. Designated as Special, Best, and Extra Special in order of alcohol content, with Special the lowest and Extra Special the highest, between 5 and 6 percent alcohol.

black and tan. A mixture of stout or porter with golden ale or lager.

bock. German for "billy goat," refers to a strong beer. A lager. In Germany a bock may be of many colors; however, outside Germany it usually means a dark beer. Bock beer averages well above 6.25 percent alcohol by volume. It is usually served seasonally, once a year, depending on what country you are in. There are many kinds of bocks, including Maibock, Doppelbock, and Weizenbock.

bottle-conditioned. Usually an ale. Yeast is added to the beer right before bottling to further the fermentation process and increase carbonation. This usually refers to a craft beer that is unpasteurized. Known in the winemaking industry as method champenoise.

bottom-fermented. How lager is brewed. Made with lager yeasts, the beer ferments at the bottom of the tun, resulting in a clearer brew than a top-fermented beer.

brewery. A place where beer is made in large quantity for sale, either retail or wholesale. The difference between a microbrewery and a brewery is that breweries produce more than 25,000 barrels of beer in any given year.

breweriana. Of or referring to beer memorabilia.

brewpub. A tavern, bar, or pub that brews its own beers. The beer is usually available on tap and, in some cases, is bottled for retail sale. Some people refer to these as microbreweries. The difference between a brewpub and a microbrewery is that a microbrewery sells larger amounts of beer and sells its beer to beer retailers.

brewer's inch. The last inch of beer in a pot or vat; the lees.

brown ale. A dark, sweet ale, usually brewed in the south of England (sweet), in the northeast of England (less sweet, reddish), and in Flanders (brown, sour). Relatively low in alcohol.

burdock. An herb once used before hops for flavoring.

buttered ale. Ale served with sugar, butter, and cinnamon.

cask-conditioned. A draft beer usually brewed in the cellar of a pub. An unpasteurized beer that goes through a secondary fermentation in the cask in which it is sold.

cauliflower. The result of the brewing of ale; the top layer of yeast.

collar. Another name for the head on the beer.

contract brew. A beer brewed for a distributor by a brewery not owned by the distributor. Usually the distributor supplies the recipe. Bottling does not necessarily take place at the brewery. Some well-known small beers are made in this fashion.

coppery. The vessels, vats, or pots that beer is brewed in; usually made of stainless steel.

cream ale. An American ale brewed with both the bottom- and top-fermentation process at the same time. This produces a light pale ale, golden in color.

dark beer. A generic term. Usually refers to a dark lager.

decoction. Style of lager determined by the way in which the malt is mashed.

deglaze. To remove the remaining bits of sautéed meat or vegetables from a pan by adding a liquid (such as beer) and heating. Used to create the base for a sauce.

Diät Pils. A beer originally brewed for diabetics. By very careful fermentation, carbohydrates are eliminated, usually resulting in a very strong beer. Germany has laws now that require many brewers of this beer to reduce the alcohol content before finishing.

doppelbock. German for "double bock." Usually very dark and sweet. An extra-strong version of bock.

Dort. Short for Dortmunder, especially in the Netherlands and Belgium.

Dortmunder. A beer brewed in Dortmund, usually of the export style.

draft beer in a can. In an attempt to create the creaminess, richness, and foaminess of draft beer, nitrogen is added to the can during canning.

dry beer. Japanese name for Diät Pils, milder than the German original, and made even more mild in America. A dry beer in America has little taste and finish.

dry hopping. When fresh hops are added to a cask of beer.

dunkel. German for "dark." Dark beers are sometimes referred to as dunkels.

eisbock. When a doppelbock beer that has been frozen and the ice is removed, the taste and alcohol level of the beverage left over is intensified.

export. A lager that usually has more body than a pilsner. The term in Germany refers to a lager that has less hops than most common pilsners. The beer is drier than a pilsner as well. Often classified as premium, which means little.

faro. A lambic beer that is sweetened by the addition of candy sugar.

fermentation. The chemical reaction whereby yeast organisms turn sugars into alcohol and carbon dioxide.

festbier. Beer made for a festival. Refers to any beer. Most of these beers are high in alcoholic content.

framboise (frambozen). A lambic made with raspberries.

fruit beer. Any lager or ale that has had fruit added to it during any stage of brewing.

genuine draft. A sterile, filtered, unpasteurized bottled or canned beer.

gravity. A weighing system used to judge the heaviness of a beer. When a beer is said to have gravity, this means that it has body and heft. In actuality, it judges the amount of hops in a beer.

grist. Barley that has been malted and milled. It is thrown in the mash tun and heated with hot water to produce the wort.

gueuze. A lambic beer that is a mixture, not necessarily in equal parts, of old and young lambic beer.

haute fermentation. French for "top fermentation."

heavy. Term used in northern England to speak of the richness and gravity of a beer.

hefe. German for "yeast." Often identifies the beer as either sedimented or that which has had yeast added to it just before bottling. See *bottle-conditioned*.

hell (or Helles). German for "pale." Generally a golden color.

hops (*humulus lupus*). The female hops plant is used in full flower to add different flavors, bitterness, and aroma to beer. In earlier times it was thought to be a preservative.

ice beer. An attempt to emulate and market an Eisbock-like beer, beer is frozen either during the fermentation process or sometime after maturation during the storage period. The water is largely removed, and then the beer is reconstituted later.

imperial stout. A stout brewed in England for the czars and sent to St. Petersburg. The alcoholic content was reportedly somewhere between 7 and 10 percent.

India pale ale. Originally a bitter beer brewed in Britain and exported to soldiers in India. It was made strong so that the beer would stand the long voyage and still be flavorful when opened halfway around the world. Today the moniker generally indicates a premium pale ale.

infusion. An English style of mashing.

kellerbier. A lager of low carbonation, very high in hops. An unfiltered beer.

kettle. Another name for the coppery, or vats, where beer is brewed.

klosterbier. German for "cloister beer." Implies that the beer was or is brewed in a convent or monastery.

Kölsch. A light ale from Cologne, Germany.

krausen. German for "crown." This is the German term for bottle-conditioning, where yeast is added just before bottling so that a higher carbonation develops in the bottle.

kriek. A lambic beer made with cherries.

kruidenbier. Dutch for "spiced beer."

kvass. A beverage very much like beer, made in Russia with rye bread.

lager. From the German word "to store." Lagers are made with a bottom- or cold-fermentation and aged for a period of up to several months to complete the fermentation. Because of their longer fermentation process, lagers are generally smoother, crisper, and more subtle in taste than ales. Lagers are always served cold. While British lager tends to be golden in color, European lagers tend to be darker. In Germany and some Dutch-speaking countries it is the term for the house beer.

lambic beer. A wheat beer, most notably from Belgium, that is fermented with wild yeasts. Finishes almost like a cider.

lamb's wool. A concoction of ales, spices, and apples.

light ale. Not to be confused with the American version of light beer, this has nothing to do with calories. In England it is the opposite of a bitter beer, usually dark. Sometimes refers to an ale with less alcoholic content, but not necessarily.

light beer. A low-calorie, low-alcohol beer. A watery version of pilsner with little flavor or body. Usually between 3 and 4 percent alcohol by content.

mailbock. A lager made in the spring to celebrate the new season; usually light in color.

malt. The basic ingredient in almost every beer. Barley that has been soaked and begins to sprout. It is then fired in a kiln and ground down. This firing process determines the color and flavor of beer.

malt liquor. Often associated with cheap beers, these tend to be American ales that range up to 7.5 percent alcohol by content. More often than not they are sweet.

Märzen (or Märzenbier). German for "March." A lager made in March for the Oktoberfest of the coming year. Usually a beer rich in malt flavors. Often amber-red in color.

mash tun. A large copper or stainless steel pot or vat.

microbrewery. A small brewery, sometimes referred to as a craft brewery. A microbrewery generally produces between 15,000 and 35,000 barrels of beer a year. Many small brewers have far exceeded that number but continue to be known as microbrewers.

mild. A beer light in hops. These are usually dark and not very high in alcoholic content.

Muenchener/Munchner. A beer-brewing style that is largely associated with Munich. These are dark lagers that are often spicy and generally not high in alcohol.

obergarig. German for "top-fermenting."

Oktoberfest. A festival in Germany that takes place in the fall; millions come every year from all over the world to take part in the festivities. It is a celebration of German history and culture—and, of course, beer. In ancient Germany the Märzenbier (the March beer) was made in March and was drunk in October to celebrate the harvests. The modern Oktoberfest lasts sixteen days, beginning in late September and ending in October. Oktoberfest found its roots in 1810 in an effort by Germans to celebrate the marriage of the crown prince of Bavaria. Smaller festivals around the world also coincide with this internationally renowned festival.

old. An English appellation given to dark beers. These beers tend to be dark and strong. They are not old in recipe or age.

oscura. Spanish for "dark beer."

pale ale. A beer lighter in color. Generally not as bitter as India pale ale. Usually ranging from golden to reddish.

pilsener/pilsner/pils. A lager or bottom-fermented beer, usually light in color. It draws its name from the town of Pilsen, in Bohemia in the Czech Republic.

The original brewer of this beer was Frantisek Poupe, and the beer, first brewed and sold in 1842, was known as Pilsner Urquell. It is a dry beer and has a wonderful hoppiness about it. The Americanized pilsner is lighter in color, flavor, and hops.

porter. Almost black, porter is a bitter, dark lager. First brewed in England around the 1730s, it got its name from the carters and porters who tended to substitute it for a meal. Porter was largely forgotten until recently. Many American microbreweries were responsible for reviving this beer.

rauchbier. A lager largely brewed in Franconia and Hamburg. The style is achieved by using smoked malts. Other variations include smoking the malt with peat moss (Scottish style) or throwing fire-heated rocks into the malt.

Reinheitsgebot. German laws that govern brewing in that country. Originally known as the Bavarian Purity Law of 1516 and now called the German Beer Purity Law. The law states that beer can only be brewed from water, hops, barley, malt, and yeast.

saison. A Belgian summer ale that is sometimes bottle-conditioned.

Schwarzbier. A beer made famous in Kostritz, Germany. A very, very dark beer.

Scotch ale. A very dark, strong ale. Many are brewed in Scotland, hence its name. Some microbreweries have begun brewing this style of beer.

shandy. A drink made of half beer and half lemonade.

steam beer. A product of the California Gold Rush, steam beer was America's first real addition to the craft of brewing. Using large shallow vats called clarifiers, lager yeast is used at high temperatures, as if one were brewing an ale. This produces a beer with the complexities of both an ale and a lager.

stout. A very dark, high-hop content ale. The most famous brewer of stout and the originator of this style is Guinness of Ireland. Stouts vary from dry to sweet, but all have sugar added to them at one stage or another. Guinness tends to be on the dry side and comes in a variety of alcoholic strengths.

top-fermented. The fermentation process used to make ale.

Trappist. A bottle-conditioned, sugar-added lager made by monks in only six breweries in the world (five in Belgium, one in Holland). While others might attempt a Trappist-style beer, only these monasteries are allowed to market their beers with this term on the label. Unusually high in alcoholic content, sometimes reaching 12 percent or more, they are fruity and some of the most highly prized beers in the world.

tripel. Dutch, meaning a brewer's strongest beer. Can be a lager, but most often is an ale.

trub. German for "sediment."

Ur-/Urquell. German for "original source." A term that means the first or original brewer; i.e., Pilsner Urqell is the original source or brewer of pilsner: the original pilsner.

Vienna. A reddish beer once made famous in Vienna, Austria. Also known as Vienna malt.

Weisse/Weissebier/Weizenbier. Wheat beer. Often served with lemon, this is an ale of extremely light color, mostly served during the summer. The beer is brewed with mainly wheat malt.

white. Another term for a wheat beer.

wiesen/weis'n. German for "meadow." This is a beer especially brewed for an occasion or a festival, like Oktoberfest.

witbier. Dutch for "white beer." Another name for white, wheat, or weisse beer.

wort. The stage in the brewing process before the addition of the yeast. The juices that result from the cooked barley.

yeast. A fungus or microorganism that causes fermentation, turning sugar into alcohol and carbon dioxide. Lager yeast is known as *Saccharommyces uvarum*, and ale yeast is known as *Saccharommces*.

zwickelbier. An unfiltered beer in Germany, usually characterless.

zymurgy. The science of brewing and fermentation, a branch of chemistry.

INDEX

Note: Page numbers in **bold** indicate recipe category lists. Recipes ending with [H] or [M] indicate high or mild alcohol warnings. [H] warnings indicate high levels of alcohol are still present; and [M] warnings indicate one or more components contain small amounts of uncooked alcohol.

A

Alcohol levels, 21–23
Ales, about, 15–16, 22. *See also* Amber ales; Blonde ales; Brown ales; Pale ales; Wheat ales/beers
Amber ales
  about: flavors of/with, 22
  Amber Ale Caramel Sauce, 62
  Amber Ale Carrot Cake with Orange Mascarpone Filling and Beer-Spiked Cream Cheese Frosting [M], 178–80
  Amber Ale Pecan Cinnamon Rolls with Beer Cream Cheese Frosting [M], 26–27
  Baked Brie with Amble Ale–Caramelized Apples and Pancetta, 44–45
  Frosted Vanilla Beer Butter Cookies [M], 192–93
  IPA Apple Fritters with Amber Ale Caramel Sauce, 194–95
Appetizers, starters and sides, **43**–59
  Baked Brie with Amble Ale–Caramelized Apples and Pancetta, 44–45
  Beer-Braised Green Beans with Shallots and Bacon, 46
  Beer Cheese Gratin Potatoes, 49
  Beer Grits with Goat Cheese and Chives, 47–48
  Chili Con Queso Cerveza Crostini, 50
  IPA Guacamole [M], 51
  Jalapeños and Bacon Beer Cheese Dip, 52
  Porter Caramelized Onion Dip [M], 54–55
  Roasted Garlic IPA Hummus [H], 53
  Roasted Garlic Pale Ale Whipped Potatoes [H], 56
  Soft Pretzels with Chipotle Beer Cheese Sauce, 57–59
Apples
  Apple Cheddar Beer Pancakes, 28–29
  Baked Brie with Amble Ale–Caramelized Apples and Pancetta, 44–45
  IPA Apple Fritters with Amber Ale Caramel Sauce, 194–95
  Saison Caramelized Apple Cake with Beer Whipped Cream [M], 204–5
Avocados
  Avocado Cream Sauce, 103
  Chili Con Queso Cerveza Crostini, 50
  IPA Guacamole [M], 51

B

Bacon and pancetta
  Baked Brie with Amble Ale–Caramelized Apples and Pancetta, 44–45
  Beer-Braised Green Beans with Shallots and Bacon, 46
  Chocolate, Bacon, and Porter Muffins, 79
  Drunken Carbonara Couscous, 81
  Jalapeños and Bacon Beer Cheese Dip, 52
  Pig Newton Beer Burgers, 123–25
Baked Brie with Amble Ale–Caramelized Apples and Pancetta, 44–45
Balsamic glazed, stout, 75
Barbecue sauce, maple stout, 73
Basil, in Creamy Pale Ale Basil Pesto Sauce [M], 64
Beans and legumes
  Beer-Braised Green Beans with Shallots and Bacon, 46
  Porter Black Bean Soup with Avocado-Cilantro Cream, 103
  Roasted Garlic IPA Hummus [H], 53
  White Bean and Beer Chicken Chili, 153
Beef, 113
  Beer-Braised Short Rib Sliders with Quick Pickled Slaw, 117
  Beer-Marinated Flank Steak with IPA Chimichurri [M], 119
  Porter Osso Buco, 129
  Slow-Roasted Maple Stout Baby Back Beef Ribs, 130–31

Steak with Stout Portobello Mushroom Sauce, 118
Stout and Stilton Beef Empanadas, 132–34
Beer and Butter Garlic Prawns, 158
Beer and Buttermilk Biscuits, 30
Beer-Braised Green Beans with Shallots and Bacon, 46
Beer-Braised Pulled-Pork Tacos with Beer Corn Tortillas, 114–16
Beer-Braised Short Rib Sliders with Quick Pickled Slaw, 117
Beer-Brined Prosciutto-Wrapped Scallops with Stout-Balsamic Glaze, 159–61
Beer-Brined Salt-Roasted Chicken, 147
Beer Cheese Gratin Potatoes, 49
Beer Cheese Sauce, 34–35, 57–59, 65
Beer Cream Cheese Frosting [M], 26–27
Beer Grits with Goat Cheese and Chives, 47–48
Beer Marinara Turkey Meatball Sandwiches, 140–41
Beer-Marinated Flank Steak with IPA Chimichurri [M], 119
Beer-Spiked Cream Cheese Frosting [M], 178–80
Beer Whipped Cream [M], 183, 196–97, 204–5
Belgian White Ale English Muffin Loaf Bread, 78
Berries
  Chocolate Raspberry Ganache, 184–86
  Strawberry Pale Ale Popsicles [H], 187
  Wheat Beer Dutch Babies, 37
Biscuits, 30
Blonde ales
  about: flavors of/with, 22
  Apple Cheddar Beer Pancakes, 28–29
  Croque Madame with Beer Cheese Sauce, 34–35
  Lobster, Corn, and Beer Chowder, 165–67
  Pilsner Coconut Curry Soup, 170–71
Bock beers
  about, 17

Pasta with Arugula, Tomatoes, and a
  Lemon-Beer Cream Sauce, 92–93
Breads, 77. *See also* Pancakes and waffles;
  Pizza and such
  Amber Ale Pecan Cinnamon Rolls with
    Beer Cream Cheese Frosting [M], 26–27
  Beer and Buttermilk Biscuits, 30
  Belgian White Ale English Muffin Loaf
    Bread, 78
  Chili Con Queso Cerveza Crostini, 50
  Chocolate, Bacon, and Porter Muffins, 79
  Classic Beer Bread, 80
  Hefeweizen Brioche Pull-Apart Dinner
    Loaf, 82–83
  Loaded Beer Corn Bread, 84
  Orange Wheat Beer and Dark Chocolate
    Muffins [M], 36
  Pale Ale Corn Tortillas, 85
  Pumpkin IPA Scones [M], 89
  Roasted Garlic and Cheddar Beer Cheese
    Muffins, 90–91
  Wheat Beer Sesame Hamburger Buns,
    96–97
Breakfast, 25–41
  Amber Ale Pecan Cinnamon Rolls with
    Beer Cream Cheese Frosting [M], 26–27
  Apple Cheddar Beer Pancakes, 28–29
  Beer and Buttermilk Biscuits, 30
  Chocolate Chip and Smoked Porter
    Pancakes, 33
  Chocolate Stout French Toast Casserole,
    31–32
  Croque Madame with Beer Cheese Sauce,
    34–35
  Orange Wheat Beer and Dark Chocolate
    Muffins [M], 36
  Pale Ale Corn Waffles with Scrambled Eggs
    and Smoky Beer Cheese Sauce, 40–41
  Sausage and Pale Ale Frittata, 38–39
  Wheat Beer Dutch Babies, 37
Brown ales
  about, 15; flavors of/with, 22
  Beer-Brined Salt-Roasted Chicken, 147
  Beer Grits with Goat Cheese and Chives,
    47–48
  Brown Ale–Brined Roast Turkey, 142–43
  Brown Sugar and Brown Ale Niçoise
    Chicken Thighs, 144–45
  Roasted Mushroom and Brown Ale Soup,
    106–7
  Salmon with Dijon Beer Cream Sauce over
    Drunken Couscous, 174–75
Brownies, chocolate stout, 182
Brown Sugar and Brown Ale Niçoise Chicken
  Thighs, 144–45
Burgers. *See* Sandwiches
Buttermilk biscuits, 30

C
Cabbage, in IPA Jalapeño Slaw [M], 126–28
Caramel sauce, 62
Carrot cake, amber ale, 178–80
Ceviche, IPA watermelon [H], 168–69
Cheese
  Apple Cheddar Beer Pancakes, 28–29
  Baked Brie with Amble Ale–Caramelized
    Apples and Pancetta, 44–45
  Beer Cheese Gratin Potatoes, 49
  Beer Cheese Sauce, 57–59
  Beer Cream Cheese Frosting [M], 26–27
  Beer Grits with Goat Cheese and Chives,
    47–48
  Beer-Spiked Cream Cheese Frosting [M],
    178–80
  Chili Con Queso Cerveza Crostini, 50
  Croque Madame with Beer Cheese Sauce,
    34–35
  Foolproof Beer Cheese Sauce, 65
  Jalapeños and Bacon Beer Cheese Dip, 52
  Lemon Pilsner Cheesecake with Beer
    Lemon Curd, 198–200
  Pale Ale Caprese Pizza, 104–5
  pasta with. *See* Pastas
  Roasted Garlic and Cheddar Beer Cheese
    Muffins, 90–91
  Saison Ricotta, Roasted Tomatoes, and
    Porter-Caramelized Shallots Galette,
    109–11
  Smoky Beer Cheese Sauce, 40–41
  Smoky Beer Mac and Cheese, 94–95
  Soft Pretzels with Chipotle Beer Cheese
    Sauce, 57–59
  Stout and Cheddar Chicken Potpies, 152
Cherries
  Chocolate Stout Mousse with Stout-Soaked
    Cherries [H], 190–91
  Stout Cherry Sauce, 122
Chicken. *See* Poultry
Chickpeas, in Roasted Garlic IPA Hummus
  [H], 53
Chili Con Queso Cerveza Crostini, 50
Chipotle Cream, 108
Chocolate
  Chocolate, Bacon, and Porter Muffins, 79
  Chocolate Chip and Smoked Porter
    Pancakes, 33
  Chocolate Porter Fudge Cookies, 181
  Chocolate Stout Brownies, 182
  Chocolate Stout Cake with Chocolate
    Raspberry Ganache and Whipped Cream
    [M], 184–86
  Chocolate Stout French Toast Casserole,
    31–32
  Chocolate Stout Fudge Sauce [H], 63

Chocolate Stout Ice Cream with Pretzels,
    188–89
  Chocolate Stout Mousse with Stout-Soaked
    Cherries [H], 190–91
  Orange Wheat Beer and Dark Chocolate
    Muffins [M], 36
Chorizo Stout Sloppy Joes, 120–21
Cilantro Lime Rice, 138–39
Cinnamon rolls, 26–27
Citrus
  Amber Ale Carrot Cake with Orange
    Mascarpone Filling and Beer-Spiked
    Cream Cheese Frosting [M], 178–80
  IPA Pavlova with Beer Lemon Curd,
    Strawberries, and Beer Whipped Cream
    [M], 196–97
  Lemon-Beer Cream Sauce, 92–93
  Lemon Orange IPA Pudding with Beer
    Whipped Cream [M], 183
  Lemon Pilsner Cheesecake with Beer
    Lemon Curd, 198–200
  Lime IPA Granita with Candied Basil [H],
    202–3
  Orange Hefeweizen Marmalade, 70–72
  Orange Wheat Beer and Dark Chocolate
    Muffins [M], 36
Classic Beer Bread, 80
Coconut, in Pilsner Coconut Curry Soup,
  170–71
Cooking with beer, 18–23. *See also specific
  recipes*
  about: overview of, 13
  alcohol levels and, 21–23
  amending recipes, 18, 19–20
  choosing beer, 18, 19
  flavor factors, 20–21, 22
  removing alcohol, 21–23
  where to start, 19
Corn
  Beer Grits with Goat Cheese and Chives,
    47–48
  Loaded Beer Corn Bread, 84
  Lobster, Corn, and Beer Chowder, 165–67
  Pale Ale Corn Tortillas, 85
Couscous
  Drunken Carbonara Couscous, 81
  Salmon with Dijon Beer Cream Sauce over
    Drunken Couscous, 174–75
Craft beer
  ales, 15–16, 22
  cooking with. *See* Cooking with beer
  defined, 12
  flavors by beer type, 22
  lagers, 17
  types of, 14–17
Creamy Pale Ale Basil Pesto Sauce [M], 64

Croque Madame with Beer Cheese Sauce, 34–35
Cucumbers, in Quick Pickled Slaw, 117
Curd, Lemon, 196–97, 198–200

D

Desserts, **177–209**
    Amber Ale Carrot Cake with Orange
        Mascarpone Filling and Beer-Spiked
        Cream Cheese Frosting [M], 178–80
    Chocolate-Chip Stout Milk Shake, 209
    Chocolate Porter Fudge Cookies, 181
    Chocolate Stout Brownies, 182
    Chocolate Stout Cake with Chocolate
        Raspberry Ganache and Whipped Cream
        [M], 184–86
    Chocolate Stout Ice Cream with Pretzels,
        188–89
    Chocolate Stout Mousse with Stout-Soaked
        Cherries [H], 190–91
    Frosted Vanilla Beer Butter Cookies [M],
        192–93
    IPA Apple Fritters with Amber Ale Caramel
        Sauce, 194–95
    IPA Pavlova with Beer Lemon Curd,
        Strawberries, and Beer Whipped Cream
        [M], 196–97
    Lemon Orange IPA Pudding with Beer
        Whipped Cream [M], 183
    Lemon Pilsner Cheesecake with Beer
        Lemon Curd, 198–200
    Lime IPA Granita with Candied Basil [H],
        202–3
    Pale Ale Pastry Dough, 201
    Saison Caramelized Apple Cake with Beer
        Whipped Cream [M], 204–5
    Strawberry Pale Ale Popsicles [H], 187
    Tropical IPA Fruit Tart, 206–7
    Vegan Pumpkin Loaf Cake [M], 208
Dijon Beer Cream Sauce, 174–75
Dips and spreads
    Chili Con Queso Cerveza Crostini, 50
    Fig Jam for Pig Newton Beer Burger, 123–25
    IPA Guacamole [M], 51
    Jalapeños and Bacon Beer Cheese Dip, 52
    Orange Hefeweizen Marmalade, 70–72
    Porter Caramelized Onion Dip [M], 54–55
    Porter Fig Jam, 74
    Roasted Garlic IPA Hummus [H], 53
Doughs. See Breads; Desserts; Pizza and such
Dressings. See Sauces
Dutch babies, wheat beer, 37

E

Eggs
    Chocolate Stout French Toast Casserole,
        31–32
    Pale Ale Corn Waffles with Scrambled Eggs
        and Smoky Beer Cheese Sauce, 40–41
    Sausage and Pale Ale Frittata, 38–39
Empanadas, 132–34

F

Fig jam, 74, 123–25
Flavor considerations, 20–21, 22
Foolproof Beer Cheese Sauce, 65
French toast casserole, chocolate stout, 31–32
Frosted Vanilla Beer Butter Cookies [M],
    192–93
Frostings. See also Whipped cream
    Beer Cream Cheese Frosting [M], 26–27
    Beer-Spiked Cream Cheese Frosting [M],
        178–80
    Chocolate Raspberry Ganache, 184–86
    for Frosted Vanilla Beer Butter Cookies [M],
        192–93
Fruit tarts, tropical IPA, 206–7
Fudge sauce, chocolate stout, 63

G

Glossary and beer terms, 210–17
Granita, lime IPA with candied basil, 202–3
Green beans, beer-braised with bacon and
    shallots, 46
Gremolata, 129
Grits, 47–48
Guacamole [M], 51

H

[H], defined, 23
Ham
    Beer-Brined Prosciutto-Wrapped Scallops
        with Stout-Balsamic Glaze, 159–61
    Croque Madame with Beer Cheese Sauce,
        34–35
Hamburger buns, 96–97
Hefeweizen
    Hefeweizen Brioche Pull-Apart Dinner
        Loaf, 82–83
    Orange Hefeweizen Marmalade, 70–72
Hollandaise sauce, 162–64
Honey Mustard Pale Ale Chicken, 146

Honey mustard vinaigrette, IPA [H], 69
Hummus [H], 53

I

Ice cream. See Desserts
IPAs
    about: flavors of, 22
    Beer-Marinated Flank Steak with IPA
        Chimichurri [M], 119
    Chili Con Queso Cerveza Crostini, 50
    IPA Apple Fritters with Amber Ale Caramel
        Sauce, 194–95
    IPA Crab Cakes with Spicy Beer
        Hollandaise, 162–64
    IPA Guacamole [M], 51
    IPA Honey Mustard Vinaigrette [H], 69
    IPA Jalapeño Slaw [M], 126–28
    IPA-Marinated Pork Chops with Stout
        Cherry Sauce, 122
    IPA Pavlova with Beer Lemon Curd,
        Strawberries, and Beer Whipped Cream
        [M], 196–97
    IPA Puttanesca Sauce [M], 66–68
    IPA Watermelon Ceviche [H], 168–69
    Lemon Orange IPA Pudding with Beer
        Whipped Cream [M], 183
    Lime IPA Granita with Candied Basil [H],
        202–3
    Paprika Chicken with Roasted Red Pepper
        Cream Sauce [M], 148–49
    Porter Fig Jam, 74
    Porter Osso Buco, 129
    Pumpkin IPA Scones [M], 89
    Roasted Garlic IPA Hummus [H], 53
    Tropical IPA Fruit Tart, 206–7
Irish Red Ale Butternut Squash Bisque with
    Goat Cheese and Pomegranate, 100–102

J

Jalapeños and Bacon Beer Cheese Dip, 52

L

Lagers, about, 17
Lemon. See Citrus
Lime IPA Granita with Candied Basil [H],
    202–3
Loaded Beer Corn Bread, 84
Lobster, Corn, and Beer Chowder, 165–67

M

[M], defined, 23
Maple and Bourbon Barrel Aged Beer–Glazed
   Salmon, 172–73
Maple Stout Barbecue Sauce, 73
Meatballs
   Beer Marinara Turkey Meatball
      Sandwiches, 140–41
   Porter-Glazed Asian Chicken Meatballs,
      150–51
Milk shake, chocolate-chip stout, 209
Muffins. See Breads
Mushrooms
   Mushroom Stout Sliders with Chipotle
      Cream, 108
   Porter, Goat Cheese, and Portobello
      Mushroom–Stuffed Pork Loin, 135
   Portobello Mushroom Sauce, 118
   Roasted Mushroom and Brown Ale Soup,
      106–7

O

Onions, in Porter Caramelized Onion Dip [M],
   54–55
Orange. See Citrus
Osso buco, porter, 129

P

Pale ales
   about, 15
   Beer and Butter Garlic Prawns, 158
   Beer and Buttermilk Biscuits, 30
   Beer-Braised Chipotle Chicken with Red
      Peppers and Onions Over Drunken
      Cilantro Lime Rice, 138–39
   Beer-Braised Green Beans with Shallots
      and Bacon, 46
   Beer Cheese Gratin Potatoes, 49
   Beer Grits with Goat Cheese and Chives,
      47–48
   Beer Marinara Turkey Meatball
      Sandwiches, 140–41
   Creamy Pale Ale Basil Pesto Sauce [M], 64
   Foolproof Beer Cheese Sauce, 65
   Honey Mustard Pale Ale Chicken, 146
   Jalapeños and Bacon Beer Cheese Dip, 52
   Lobster, Corn, and Beer Chowder, 165–67
   Pale Ale Caprese Pizza, 104–5
   Pale Ale Corn Tortillas, 85
   Pale Ale Corn Waffles with Scrambled Eggs
      and Smoky Beer Cheese Sauce, 40–41
   Pale Ale Pasta Cavatelli, 86–87
   Pale Ale Pastry Dough, 201

   Pasta with Arugula, Tomatoes, and a
      Lemon-Beer Cream Sauce, 92–93
   Pilsner Coconut Curry Soup, 170–71
   Roasted Garlic and Cheddar Beer Cheese
      Muffins, 90–91
   Roasted Garlic Pale Ale Whipped Potatoes
      [H], 56
   Sausage and Pale Ale Frittata, 38–39
   Smoky Beer Mac and Cheese, 94–95
   Strawberry Pale Ale Popsicles [H], 187
   Tropical IPA Fruit Tart, 206–7
   White Bean and Beer Chicken Chili, 153
Pale lagers, about, 17
Pancakes and waffles
   Apple Cheddar Beer Pancakes, 28–29
   Chocolate Chip and Smoked Porter
      Pancakes, 33
   Chocolate Stout French Toast Casserole,
      31–32
   Pale Ale Corn Waffles with Scrambled Eggs
      and Smoky Beer Cheese Sauce, 40–41
   Wheat Beer Dutch Babies, 37
Paprika Chicken with Roasted Red Pepper
   Cream Sauce [M], 148–49
Pastas, 77
   Drunken Carbonara Couscous, 81
   Pale Ale Pasta Cavatelli, 86–87
   Pasta with Arugula, Tomatoes, and a
      Lemon-Beer Cream Sauce, 92–93
   sauces for. See Sauces
   Smoky Beer Mac and Cheese, 94–95
Pavlovas, IPA, 196–97
Peppers
   Beer-Braised Chipotle Chicken with Red
      Peppers and Onions Over Drunken
      Cilantro Lime Rice, 138–39
   IPA Jalapeño Slaw [M], 126–28
   IPA Puttanesca Sauce [M], 66–68
   Jalapeños and Bacon Beer Cheese Dip, 52
   Roasted Red Pepper Cream Sauce [M],
      148–49
Pesto sauce, 64
Pig Newton Beer Burgers, 123–25
Pilsners
   about, 17; flavors of, 22
   Apple Cheddar Beer Pancakes, 28–29
   Lemon Pilsner Cheesecake with Beer
      Lemon Curd, 198–200
   Lobster, Corn, and Beer Chowder, 165–67
   Pale Ale Pastry Dough, 201
   Pilsner Coconut Curry Soup, 170–71
Pizza and such
   Pale Ale Caprese Pizza, 104–5
   Saison Ricotta, Roasted Tomatoes, and
      Porter-Caramelized Shallots Galette,
      109–11

Popsicles, strawberry pale ale, 187
Pork, 113. See also Bacon and pancetta
   Beer-Braised Pulled-Pork Tacos with Beer
      Corn Tortillas, 114–16
   Beer-Brined Prosciutto-Wrapped Scallops
      with Stout-Balsamic Glaze, 159–61
   Chorizo Stout Sloppy Joes, 120–21
   Croque Madame with Beer Cheese Sauce,
      34–35
   IPA-Marinated Pork Chops with Stout
      Cherry Sauce, 122
   Pig Newton Beer Burgers, 123–25
   Porter, Goat Cheese, and Portobello
      Mushroom–Stuffed Pork Loin, 135
   Porter-Braised Pulled-Pork Sandwiches
      with IPA Jalapeño Slaw [M], 126–28
   Sausage and Pale Ale Frittata, 38–39
Porters. See also Stouts
   about: baking with, 31; flavors of, 22; stouts
      and, 16, 31
   Chocolate, Bacon, and Porter Muffins, 79
   Chocolate Chip and Smoked Porter
      Pancakes, 33
   Chocolate Porter Fudge Cookies, 181
   Chocolate Stout French Toast Casserole,
      31–32
   Porter, Goat Cheese, and Portobello
      Mushroom–Stuffed Pork Loin, 135
   Porter Black Bean Soup with Avocado-
      Cilantro Cream, 103
   Porter-Braised Pulled-Pork Sandwiches
      with IPA Jalapeño Slaw [M], 126–28
   Porter Caramelized Onion Dip [M], 54–55
   Porter Fig Jam, 74
   Porter-Glazed Asian Chicken Meatballs,
      150–51
   Saison Ricotta, Roasted Tomatoes, and
      Porter-Caramelized Shallots Galette,
      109–11
   Vegan Pumpkin Loaf Cake [M], 208
Portobello Mushroom Sauce, 118
Potatoes
   Beer Cheese Gratin Potatoes, 49
   Roasted Garlic Pale Ale Whipped Potatoes
      [H], 56
Potpies, chicken, 152
Poultry, 137–55
   Beer-Braised Chipotle Chicken with Red
      Peppers and Onions Over Drunken
      Cilantro Lime Rice, 138–39
   Beer-Brined Salt-Roasted Chicken, 147
   Beer Marinara Turkey Meatball
      Sandwiches, 140–41
   Brown Ale–Brined Roast Turkey, 142–43
   Brown Sugar and Brown Ale Niçoise
      Chicken Thighs, 144–45
   Honey Mustard Pale Ale Chicken, 146

Paprika Chicken with Roasted Red Pepper Cream Sauce [M], 148–49
Porter-Glazed Asian Chicken Meatballs, 150–51
Stout and Cheddar Chicken Potpies, 152
Stout and Pomegranate–Glazed Chicken Wings, 154–55
White Bean and Beer Chicken Chili, 153
Prawns. *See* Seafood
Pretzels
Chocolate Stout Ice Cream with Pretzels, 188–89
Soft Pretzels with Chipotle Beer Cheese Sauce, 57–59
Pumpkin and pumpkin ale
Pumpkin IPA Scones [M], 89
Vegan Pumpkin Loaf Cake [M], 208
Puttanesca Sauce [M], 66–68

Q

Quick Pickled Slaw, 117

R

Raspberries. *See* Berries
Recipes. *See also* Cooking with beer
amending, by substituting beer, 18, 19–20
choosing beer for, 18, 19. *See also specific recipes*
fat considerations, 19
flavor factors, 20–21, 22
Red ale, in Irish Red Ale Butternut Squash Bisque with Goat Cheese and Pomegranate, 100–102
Rice, cilantro lime, 138–39
Roasted Garlic and Cheddar Beer Cheese Muffins, 90–91
Roasted Garlic IPA Hummus [H], 53
Roasted Garlic Pale Ale Whipped Potatoes [H], 56
Roasted Mushroom and Brown Ale Soup, 106–7
Roasted Red Pepper Cream Sauce [M], 148–49

S

Saisons
Saison Caramelized Apple Cake with Beer Whipped Cream [M], 204–5
Saison Ricotta, Roasted Tomatoes, and Porter-Caramelized Shallots Galette, 109–11

Salad dressings. *See* Sauces
Salads
IPA Jalapeño Slaw [M], 126–28
Quick Pickled Slaw, 117
Salmon. *See* Seafood
Sandwiches
Beer Marinara Turkey Meatball Sandwiches, 140–41
Chorizo Stout Sloppy Joes, 120–21
Mushroom Stout Sliders with Chipotle Cream, 108
Pig Newton Beer Burgers, 123–25
Porter-Braised Pulled-Pork Sandwiches with IPA Jalapeño Slaw [M], 126–28
Sauces, **61**–75
Avocado Cream Sauce, 103
Beer Cheese Sauce, 34–35, 57–59
Beer Marinara, 140–41
Chipotle Cream, 108
Creamy Pale Ale Basil Pesto Sauce [M], 64
Dijon Beer Cream Sauce, 174–75
Foolproof Beer Cheese Sauce, 65
IPA Honey Mustard Vinaigrette [H], 69
IPA Puttanesca Sauce [M], 66–68
Lemon-Beer Cream Sauce, 92–93
Maple Stout Barbecue Sauce, 73
Porter Fig Jam, 74
Portobello Mushroom Sauce, 118
Roasted Red Pepper Cream Sauce [M], 148–49
Smoky Beer Cheese Sauce, 40–41
Spicy Beer Hollandaise, 162–64
Stout-Balsamic Glaze, 75
Stout Balsamic Glaze, 159–61
Stout Cherry Sauce, 122
Tomatillo Chimichurri, 119
Sauces, sweet. *See also* Frostings; Whipped cream
Amber Ale Caramel Sauce, 62
Amber Ale Carmel Sauce, 195
Chocolate Stout Fudge Sauce [H], 63
Orange Hefeweizen Marmalade, 70–72
Sausage
Chorizo Stout Sloppy Joes, 120–21
Sausage and Pale Ale Frittata, 38–39
Scones, pumpkin [M], 89
Seafood, **157**–75
Beer and Butter Garlic Prawns, 158
Beer-Brined Prosciutto-Wrapped Scallops with Stout-Balsamic Glaze, 159–61
IPA Crab Cakes with Spicy Beer Hollandaise, 162–64
IPA Watermelon Ceviche [H], 168–69
Lobster, Corn, and Beer Chowder, 165–67

Maple and Bourbon Barrel Aged Beer-Glazed Salmon, 172–73
Pilsner Coconut Curry Soup, 170–71
Salmon with Dijon Beer Cream Sauce over Drunken Couscous, 174–75
Shrimp. *See* Seafood
Slaw. *See* Salads
Sliders, mushroom stout, 108
Sloppy Joes, 120–21
Slow-Roasted Maple Stout Baby Back Beef Ribs, 130–31
Smoky Beer Cheese Sauce, 40–41
Smoky Beer Mac and Cheese, 94–95
Soft Pretzels with Chipotle Beer Cheese Sauce, 57–59
Soups and stews
Irish Red Ale Butternut Squash Bisque with Goat Cheese and Pomegranate, 100–102
Lobster, Corn, and Beer Chowder, 165–67
Pilsner Coconut Curry Soup, 170–71
Porter Black Bean Soup with Avocado-Cilantro Cream, 103
Roasted Mushroom and Brown Ale Soup, 106–7
White Bean and Beer Chicken Chili, 153
Spicy Beer Hollandaise, 162–64
Spreads. *See* Dips and spreads
Squash bisque, 100–102
Steak with Stout Portobello Mushroom Sauce, 118
Stouts. *See also* Porters
about: baking with, 31; flavors of, 22; porters and, 16, 31
Beer-Braised Pulled-Pork Tacos with Beer Corn Tortillas, 114–16
Beer-Braised Short Rib Sliders with Quick Pickled Slaw, 117
Beer-Brined Prosciutto-Wrapped Scallops with Stout-Balsamic Glaze, 159–61
Chocolate-Chip Stout Milk Shake, 209
Chocolate Stout Brownies, 182
Chocolate Stout Cake with Chocolate Raspberry Ganache and Whipped Cream [M], 184–86
Chocolate Stout French Toast Casserole, 31–32
Chocolate Stout Fudge Sauce [H], 63
Chocolate Stout Ice Cream with Pretzels, 188–89
Chocolate Stout Mousse with Stout-Soaked Cherries [H], 190–91
Chorizo Stout Sloppy Joes, 120–21
Fig Jam for Pig Newton Beer Burger, 123–25

Maple and Bourbon Barrel Aged Beer–
    Glazed Salmon, 172–73
Maple Stout Barbecue Sauce, 73
Mushroom Stout Sliders with Chipotle
    Cream, 108
Slow-Roasted Maple Stout Baby Back Beef
    Ribs, 130–31
Steak with Stout Portobello Mushroom
    Sauce, 118
Stout and Cheddar Chicken Potpies, 152
Stout and Pomegranate–Glazed Chicken
    Wings, 154–55
Stout and Stilton Beef Empanadas, 132–34
Stout-Balsamic Glaze, 75
Stout Cherry Sauce, 122
Vegan Pumpkin Loaf Cake [M], 208
Strawberries. *See* Berries

T

Tomatillo Chimichurri, 119
Tomatoes
    Beer Marinara, 140–41
    IPA Puttanesca Sauce [M], 66–68
    pasta with. *See* Pastas
    Saison Ricotta, Roasted Tomatoes, and
        Porter-Caramelized Shallots Galette,
        109–11
Tortillas
    Beer-Braised Pulled-Pork Tacos with Beer
        Corn Tortillas, 114–16
    Pale Ale Corn Tortillas, 85
Tropical IPA Fruit Tart, 206–7
Turkey. *See* Poultry

V

Vegan Pumpkin Loaf Cake [M], 208
Veggie lovers entrées, **99**–111
    Irish Red Ale Butternut Squash Bisque with
        Goat Cheese and Pomegranate, 100–102
    Mushroom Stout Sliders with Chipotle
        Cream, 108
    Pale Ale Caprese Pizza, 104–5
    Porter Black Bean Soup with Avocado-
        Cilantro Cream, 103
    Roasted Mushroom and Brown Ale Soup,
        106–7
    Saison Ricotta, Roasted Tomatoes, and
        Porter-Caramelized Shallots Galette,
        109–11
Vinaigrette, IPA honey mustard [H], 69

W

Waffles. *See* Pancakes and waffles
Watermelon ceviche [H], 168–69
Wheat ales/beers. *See also* Hefeweizen
    about, 16; flavors of/with, 22
    Beer-Braised Green Beans with Shallots
        and Bacon, 46
    Beer-Braised Pulled-Pork Tacos with Beer
        Corn Tortillas, 114–16
    Belgian White Ale English Muffin Loaf
        Bread, 78
    Classic Beer Bread, 80
    Loaded Beer Corn Bread, 84
    Orange Wheat Beer and Dark Chocolate
        Muffins [M], 36
    Pale Ale Pastry Dough, 201
    Pig Newton Beer Burgers, 123–25
    Saison Ricotta, Roasted Tomatoes, and
        Porter-Caramelized Shallots Galette,
        109–11
    Soft Pretzels with Chipotle Beer Cheese
        Sauce, 57–59
    Wheat Beer Dutch Babies, 37
    Wheat Beer Sesame Hamburger Buns,
        96–97
Whipped cream, 183, 184, 196–97, 204–5
White ale
    Drunken Carbonara Couscous, 81
    Wheat Beer Dutch Babies, 37
White Bean and Beer Chicken Chili, 153

ABOUT the AUTHOR

JACQUELYN DODD is a Los Angeles–based recipe developer, food photographer, and food writer. She runs the popular cooking-with-beer website *www.TheBeeroness.com*, creating recipes with craft beer as well as giving readers craft beer reviews. She also writes recipes, articles, and restaurant reviews for the popular websites SheKnows and Honest Cooking, as well as the print magazine *Whisk*. Additionally, Jackie is a highly sought after freelance photographer who uses her skills to photograph beer, food, architecture, restaurants, and bars in Southern California. She has appeared on NPR and *The Today Show* as well as CBS LA (*www.losangeles.cbslocal.com/2012/08/31/the-beeroness-brews-up-a-new-twist-on-everday-recipes/*), giving unique recipes that feature craft beer.